THE
MAMMOTH
LETTERS

Running Away to a
Mountain Town

Jennifer K. Crittenden

WHISTLING
RABBIT
PRESS

The Mammoth Letters: Running Away to a Mountain Town
by Jennifer K. Crittenden
Copyright © 2017 Jennifer K. Crittenden

Published by
Whistling Rabbit Press
San Diego, California
whistlingrabbitpress.com
Contact the publisher at info@whistlingrabbit.com.
Additional materials are available at mammothletters.com.

Charitable donation: A one dollar donation will be made to the Southern Mono Historical Society with each purchase of a new paperback.

Cover design by Damonza
Interior design by Damonza
Illustrations on pages 38, 62, and 172 by Kira Hirsch
Illustrations on pages 82, 128, 218 by Melanie Taylor
Author photograph by Tom Harvey
Map by Tom Harvey using map background by Stamen Design (stamen.com), under creativecommons.org/licenses/by/3.0, data by openstreetmap.org under ODbL.

Absens et Indagans was previously serialized in the *Mammoth Times* in modified form.

Excerpts from Alsup, William *Missing in the Minarets: The Search for Walter A. Starr, Jr. Yosemite National Park*, CA: Yosemite Association, 2001 are used with kind permission from the Yosemite Conservancy.

Printed in the United States of America

Publisher's Cataloging-in-Publication data

Crittenden, Jennifer K.
    The Mammoth letters : running away to a mountain town / Jennifer K. Crittenden
    p. cm.
    ISBN 978-0-9847360-8-9 (pbk.)
    ISBN 978-0-9847360-9-6 (e-book)
    Includes index.
    1. Mammoth Lakes (Calif.)—Description. 2. Sierra Nevada (Calif. and Nev.)—Description. 3. Sierra Nevada (Calif. And Nev.)—History. 4. Mammoth Lakes (Calif.)—Social life and customs. 5. Writers—United States—Biography. I. Title.

F869.M275C 2017
979.4 —dc23   2017948972

To the people of the Eastern Sierra and to those who cherish it, near and far

CONTENTS

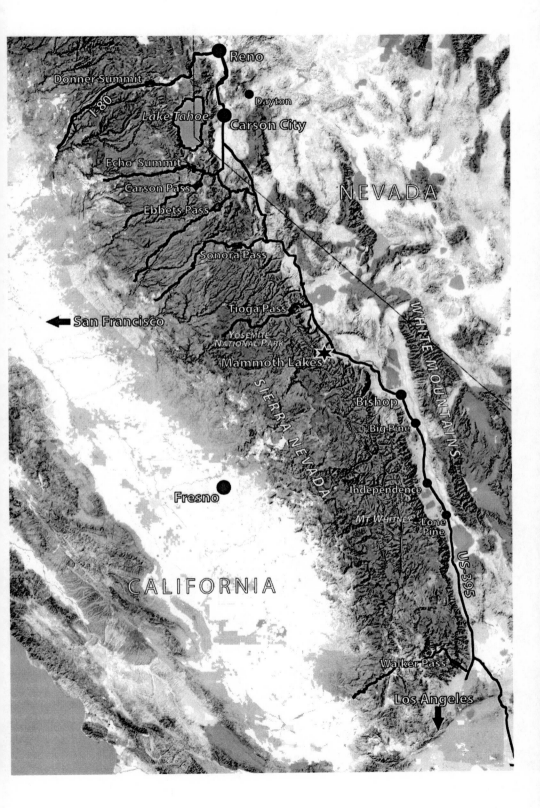

INTRODUCTION

I just looked, nothing more...
Then I got so full of looking that I had to write to
get rid of some of it and make room for more.

~ MARY AUSTIN

THIS IS NOT the book I intended to write.

My family and I had moved from the coastal community of
Del Mar near San Diego, California, to Mammoth Lakes for a
serious change of scenery. Mammoth Lakes is a small town well-
known for its ski resort; it's located at 8,000 feet in the Eastern Sierra,
forty miles from the next town. Julian, my twelve-year-old son, had
fallen in love with snowboarding, and my husband and I were reluctant city dwellers, despite twenty years in Southern California, and
yearned for a change of pace. We expected to stay for a year—Julian
would attend a new and different kind of school, and I would work
on my third book. Luc, my nineteen-year-old son, was attending the
University of California, Santa Cruz, and would visit during breaks.

Once at altitude, I did begin writing—but the wrong stuff was
coming out. I had intended to write a sports-related book, but,
inspired by my new surroundings, I began sending narrative letters

to friends and family about the area and our experiences in the community. As the beauty and history of the Eastern Sierra drew me in, I learned other stories—of adventure and animals, of politics and human nature, of courage and tragedy—that combined with my own journals would offer an introduction to a place that other reluctant city dwellers may dream about.

Living in Mammoth Lakes full time was a joy, and my appreciation for its special community continues to grow. We loved becoming part of the local scene, and I cannot adequately express my gratitude for the warm welcome we received. To protect the innocent (and the not-so-innocent), except for cases when I was given specific permission to use someone's name or when someone's name was already in the public sphere, I have omitted or changed the names of the individuals who appear in the book.

A comment here about truth and accuracy: the activities, dialogue, events, quotes, and actions involving my personal life are all true. For the factual information in the book, I drew from existing books, conversations with those involved, Wikipedia, and a multitude of online and written sources. I attempted to make the reporting as accurate as possible, and many experts were kind enough to review and correct my work, as noted in the acknowledgments. Nevertheless, any errors are my own responsibility.

As it turned out, I had too much material for one book, so look for more *Mammoth Letters* in the future. Other excellent books that expand on the topics I cover here exist, and it is my hope that this book will inspire more interest in the Eastern Sierra. I encourage you to use the notes and bibliography at the end of the book to dive in deeper.

DEPARTURE AND ARRIVAL

Faeries, come take me out of this dull world,
For I would ride with you upon the wind,
Run on the top of the dishevelled tide,
And dance upon the mountains like a flame.

~ W. B. YEATS, *THE LAND OF HEART'S DESIRE*

August 18–23, 2014

Monday

WE ROSE WITH high hopes of leaving Del Mar, California, mid-morning, but those hopes faded over the hours of "last-minute" packing, cleaning, laundry, making the beds, emptying the refrigerator, and packing the cars. Wrapping our clothes and belongings in the garage in plastic drop cloths so that our house would be ready for the tenants was very time consuming and sweaty. But we made it. My brother had said it wasn't possible, and he was nearly right.

My husband, Tom, worked his usual miracles in car packing, finding room for an enormous plank for my writing desk, endless boxes and bags, nine computers (I think), and six cameras (ditto)—but only two bikes (most of them were already in Mammoth). We finally left at 2:32 p.m. in two cars. My older son, Luc, and I raced ahead up I-15, cranking tunes from my tape deck (which still worked, provoking my son to roll his eyes). High spirits and excitement (and caffeine) fueled us through San Bernardino and Kramer Junction. Several hours later, we reunited with Tom and my younger son, Julian, in the other car when we stopped to look at the amazing blood-red sunset along a smoky section of US 395. It turned out that a Yosemite fire that had started several weeks before was still burning.

It had been a very hot drive; sunset brought relief from the solar heating, but the outside temperature was still very high, surely over ninety degrees. Being gas conscious, Luc refused to turn on the AC, so I secretly turned it on when he dozed, a transgression that he rectified the moment he woke up. In our rush to depart, all the snacks had ended up in the other car, and we finally talked Tom and Julian into stopping at Carl's Jr. in Bishop. Since it was now 9:30 at night, the food tasted delicious. Cheerful and revived, we set off on the last leg up the hill to Mammoth. When we stepped out of the car, a chilly wind hit us, swooshing in the trees high above us. "I'm cold," Luc said immediately, and I grabbed a jacket. We had arrived.

Tuesday

We awoke with big plans. The house in Mammoth has been used as a vacation house by Tom and his siblings for over twenty years, but without full-time occupants, it has fallen into disrepair. Finally, we have time to fix it up. First, we tumbled the kids out of bed to push an old Subaru out of the garage and around a corner into the circular driveway. Fortunately, no one got run over. Hours of unpacking then ensued while I attacked the kitchen. Gradually, the spider-webby, grimy chaos, questionable-looking spots, mysterious jars lurking in dark corners, and a refrigerator with secrets gave way to shelf paper, shiny counters, and organization. Upon request, Tom brought me a huge metal trash can that I filled twice. The only downside was Tom kept pulling expired food out of the trash can and claiming that he would eat it. So I was able to get rid of only one of the four boxes of expired instant oatmeal, a repellent food even before it expires.

I stopped by Mammoth Middle School to sign the rest of the paperwork to enroll Julian, my twelve-year-old son. The secretary handed me a stream of rules and policies to sign but not read. She was bright and cheerful throughout, and I tried to be.

The office was busy with students and families, mostly Latino, getting enrolled, asking questions, and going in and out for mysterious reasons. All of the conversations on my side of the desk were in Spanish. The district superintendent stopped by, and an office worker complained that thirty-five children still had not enrolled—how she knew that, I'm not sure, but it is a small community. I learned the school enrollment was up to nearly three hundred now, across three grades.

While I was waiting, a heavyset girl with black braids wrapped around her head (which appears to be the mandatory hair style this year) came to the desk and explained that she was not yet registered. An administrator glared at her.

"Why not?" she demanded. The girl faltered and glanced helplessly toward the hall.

"My mom is here," she said.

The administrator sighed and brought out the paperwork. The process seemed surprisingly personal and manual. No one said a word about proof of residency, a telling difference from the process in the Del Mar school district we'd just left where it is all about the residency.

My prize for all this was a printed copy of Julian's schedule. He's in advanced Math! And he has Spanish, alternating with Exercise Science (yet another euphemism for Gym). He also has something called "Art thru Writin," which sounds like it should go in a John Prine song: *Move to the country, eat a lot of peaches, find art thru writin', on your own.* I carefully brought home the schedule along with a map of the town, and Julian and I studied it over dinner of BBQ ribs and salad.

Wednesday

The big day! Julian announced before we left the house that he was excited about the bike ride but scared about school. He looked pretty sharp on his bike, riding down on the bike path, under the pines and along the golf course. Tom and I rode with him, also excited to be able to ride to school, a near impossibility in our town in Southern California. After I took off my helmet, Julian allowed me to nip into the office to tell a staff member that Julian's paperwork still listed his gender as "F"(!). She didn't seem very concerned. Julian and I made the requisite jokes about appearing in the girls' locker room for Exercise Science. "Ooooh," he squeaked in a fake falsetto.

"It's like that story *There's a Boy in the Girls' Bathroom*," I said.

"No, Mom," he said, "it *is* that story."

The entrance foyer was jammed with kids in backpacks, chattering and grinning. Julian disappeared in the direction of his first class. Surveying the crowd, I would have guessed the school was more than 50 percent Hispanic. That was one of the reasons I was interested in having Julian attend the school. Here are the official school stats compared to those of the school Julian would have attended back home.

Mammoth Lakes:

287 students, 18:1 student/teacher ratio, 38 percent white, 45 percent eligible for free lunch, $11,311 district spending per student

Del Mar:

702 students, 24:1 student/teacher ratio, 73 percent white, 4 percent eligible for free lunch, $9,458 district spending per student

Those differences don't necessarily mean one school is superior, but at least Mammoth is different; the middle school back home would have been very similar to Julian's elementary school.

Loitering outside the school after the bell had rung, Tom and I eavesdropped on the welcome address and the pledge of allegiance. The speakers congratulated the sixth graders on finding their classrooms and made some whooping noises about school pride. Their school mascot is the mountain lion, which is odd because the elementary school kids are called the Husky Pups, and the high schoolers the Huskies. Apparently the middle schoolers are a different species—on second thought, maybe that makes sense.

Tom and I rode back along Mammoth Creek, a very beautiful ride through the meadow with a fantastic view of the mountains. The creek is not one of those weak-assed trickles of the low country; it is a robust, rushing force, tearing through the underbrush and ripping along the banks. We crossed several bridges as we meandered our way back through a neighborhood off Old Mammoth Road, one with aspirations of grandeur, although most of the people I saw appeared to be living more of a camping lifestyle.

At this time of year, during the off-season, the presence of cars, or lack thereof, distinguish the vacation homes from the locals' residences, which in large part consist of condos, apartments, or small houses. Subarus, trucks, dogs, and coffee mugs set out on picnic tables are all signs of permanent residents. The second-home McMansions look abandoned. It's easy to see the difference between the haves and the have-nots here. The wonderful bike ride, however, raised a question—*today, on this lovely, sunny morning, who is wealthier?*

We followed the path along banks of flowers and grasses, sparkling with dew. The sun was higher, and it had started to warm up. Traffic had grown on Old Mammoth Road, and more people were out running and walking.

After a cup of coffee at home, I headed down to get my hair cut.

"How did you pick the salon?" my husband asked.

"It was the first one I saw," I admitted.

May, my haircutter, comes a bit late and blames the "traffic" for her tardiness. She lives in June Lake and went to cosmetology school in suburban San Diego. She complains a lot—about people who don't care about their hair, about people who show up the night before school starts to get their kid's hair cut, about the anti-development attitudes of the June Lake residents ("if there's no reason for people to go there, it's going to turn into Bodie"), but I enjoy her conversation. She says some amazing things that I don't believe: the Mammoth Vons is the highest-grossing Vons in the country, there's a 2 percent tourist tax tacked onto everything you buy at Vons, and more people come to Mammoth in the summer than the winter ("they come here to get away from the heat"). But some things she said I do believe: people drive nearly three hours to go to the Costco in Carson City, Mammoth Lakes has eight thousand people, and local kids try to go to Mammoth High School instead of to the surrounding schools. As it would turn out, she was right about the summer visitation but not about Vons or the 2 percent tax.

Partway through my meticulous and reasonably priced haircut, Anna, another stylist, appears. She announces that she is not a complainer, but painters left paint chips all over outside her apartment building and her window is stuck shut now. She walks around us, wondering out loud if she should call to complain, even though she's not a complainer. She finally picks up the phone and calls the property manager's number and reaches someone she apparently knows. She leads with the stuck window which goes badly as the person on the other end tells her she needs to pay for a maintenance visit. She then complains about having had to pay to have the carpets cleaned and asks about the paint chips whereupon the person on the other end apparently hangs up on her. Poor Anna. She stands behind us with tears in her eyes and says, "I shouldn't have called. Now I'm upset." She recounts the conversation at length, and I nod or shake my head at various intervals as seems appropriate.

May says, "That's so annoying," at least six times. At one point, she whispers to me, "She just needs to use a razor blade to get that window open." I nod conspiratorially.

Another customer shows up; she looks as though she has just rolled out from cleaning the basement. I keep being surprised by that up here—some people really don't care how they look. The new client is outspoken and bright-eyed.

"Look at all that hair!" she exclaims over my gray-brown curls on the floor. "I would give my eyeteeth to have curly hair." I glance surreptitiously at her hair. It is a bit flat and wispy and white and very short. It dawns on me that she doesn't really look as though she needs a haircut. Maybe she comes because it's the social thing to do.

We asked Julian the usual questions after the first day of school. He had a corn dog and Tater Tots for lunch.

"That's all?" I said, surprised.

"Well, and chocolate milk," he said.

I asked if he had found anyone to have lunch with.

"Oh, yeah," he said breezily. "I have three friends now." He said that two are identical twins. "I'm the only one who can tell them apart," he said.

"How do you do that?" I asked.

"One wears braces," he said.

Thursday

Like his son, Tom is gas conscious and happy to be living in a town with lots of bike paths so we can leave the cars parked more often. He brought the trash with us this morning in the bike trailer to take to the transfer station, and he received lots of smiles along the bike path. Either people thought he had a baby in there, or they were very approving of carrying trash around in a bike trailer. Most of the kids and moms walking and biking to school were Latino, and there was lots of Spanish heard on the paths. More white kids arrived in cars, many in Subarus and Jeeps. I haven't seen a single Bimmer or Mercedes since we've gotten to Mammoth. There was also no drop-off insanity as there was at our Southern California school when too many large vehicles crammed into too small a space in too short of a time. Could it be because they actually run a bus system in Mammoth?

After leaving Julian at school, we rode past the elementary school where there was also a small drop-off line. The schools' start times are staggered, which is sensible given that the schools—elementary, middle, and high—are all right in a row. We then rode along a charming meandering trail over to Main Street and took the bike path up to the post office where mail was waiting for us!

After the climb back home following school drop off, I lost my mind and ate a donut. So much for the healthy mountain lifestyle. I *must* get a scale.

Julian reported that he had chicken and salad for lunch, that the school has a kitchen right there in the gymnasium, and that they actually cook food on site—a throwback to the hot school fare I was served in my day that I thought had disappeared from modern life. He came home this afternoon after a pretty long ride with Tom and announced that he had homework.

"I can't believe I'm excited about homework," he muttered.

Friday

I appreciate how dark it is here at night. In Del Mar, our neighbors installed a piercing outside light, perhaps to compensate for the lack of street lights. When I'd get up in the night and that thing would hit me in the eye, I couldn't help but feel offended. Here, there is more respect for the night sky. One neighbor has a low light outside his door, but otherwise it is pitch black and stars fill the sky like strewn diamonds.

The wind picked up during the night, and it was blowing pretty hard this morning—what you might call *bracing*—when we set off on our way to school. Tom is excited to be in a place with weather. He keeps running off to the Internet to see what's happening outside. We noticed a harbinger of weather to come this morning when ten-foot-high snow poles showed up, marking the walkway to the school. They seemed to say, "Enjoy your mild weather while it's here…"

Yesterday, after leaving the post office, we found another great bike path through the so-called "ghetto," the old part of town. I think of it as the smoky zone, having gone running through there some years ago and nearly asphyxiating. The town has worked to replace wood-burning stoves with pellet stoves using funds from a state grant, but wood-burning stoves were grandfathered in for older houses. The path also runs through a wooded area beside a series of vacant lots that Tom speculated had been laid out but then abandoned after the real estate bubble burst. It looked like great bear country to me, so I kept an eye out.

Today after dropping Julian at school, we cut over to Main Street on the road that runs past the hospital and rode up Forest Trail through an area full of old cabins and A-frames. As we tooled around the tennis courts, a man in a pickup stopped and called to us, "There's a bear over there!" I did see something brown and round and moving in the distance that could have been a bear. Since we're going everywhere on bikes now, we may have to sprint!

There was a story in the paper yesterday about a bear who broke into two kitchens and a car. In the first house, the couple was home; they ran into the kitchen yelling, "Bad bear!" and had the presence of mind to gather two pan lids and bang them together to run him off. He jumped out the kitchen window, taking the screen with him, and then stood on his hind feet and put his face back in the window and looked at them. On his way to the next house, he smashed into a car and checked out a backpack. He made a heck of a mess in the second kitchen where no one was home; the house was unlocked, so a local bear authority entered and discovered the bear sitting in the hallway eating a ham. The bear ran away, but he had been marked with green and yellow ear tags, and we now know that he was a Nevada bear. The bear official described the bear as smart and "cute as the dickens," but said he has to go out and live on natural food now. "He can't just go around breaking into kitchens," he said. The paper advised everyone to keep downstairs windows closed. *Can you imagine?*

Having seen a "For Sale" photo of some bookcases pinned up at the post office, I called to inquire if they were still available.

"Yep, they are," the woman responded. "But you gotta come now because I gotta get going. Got things to do."

We hurriedly headed back to Forest Trail. The bookcases were a bit rickety, so Tom and I hemmed and hawed as we talked with the owner. She was a brusque, friendly, lumpy mountain type—not pretty to look at but entertaining.

"Bought this house off my old boyfriend for thirty-five thousand, sixteen years ago," she announced as she bustled around. "Pretty good deal. 'Course I did a lot of work on it—put a new roof on it and fixed the driveway, which was coming up in chunks."

Much of the conversation focused on money.

"Put sixty thousand into it," she said. "Got a buddy of mine to work for twenty dollars an hour even though he had just got his contractor's license."

Her house is a tidy brown-shingled affair with a metal roof, two steeples, and a sliding glass front door. I openly admired it and her clean garage.

"Had a garage sale," she said proudly. "Made three hundred and fifty bucks. And got eight hundred for my flatbed trailer." I also commented on her lush green lawn and noticed again that the locals do not refer to themselves as locals or natives. They call themselves "people who live here."

"People who live here have lawns," she announced in blatant disregard for the lack of lawns in each direction as far as the eye could see in front of houses clearly inhabited by people who live here as evidenced by their visible vehicles, snow blowers, and dogs.

"You just moved here?" she said, eyeing us, but not really very curious about us.

"Sweet!" she trilled when I handed over two fifties. Then she trundled off to her truck with her two dogs in tow.

People like us come and go.

It was during a previous August visit that I first noticed the locals. During ski season, they are hidden like rare birds among the sparkling twittering Southern Californians who descend on Vons, grabbing cheese and wine, calling out to each other, and generally making a racket. When the tourists' migration season is over, the natives emerge, a bushy-haired, rough-looking people in boots and Subarus. Their skin toughened by sun and wind and perhaps a shot or two of Jack, they would not make good poster children for plastic surgeons.

"They look like Oregonians," I told a friend.

She chuckled and said, "You ever notice how there are never any calendars for the Men of Oregon?"

They know about bears and blizzards and how to jump-start a car and troubleshoot a snowblower. Mammoth writer, George Shirk, said in an article in the *Utne Reader* that there are three kinds of locals: runaways, athletes, and "dreamers."

People in town usually say "hi" to each other, particularly if you're in a place where tourists are less likely to roam—the school, the DIY center, the post office. One guy greeted me so enthusiastically in the cookie aisle at Vons I thought I must actually know him. Lots of people do know each other, and you pick up local cultural tidbits by eavesdropping.

"Gotta buy a new saw. Gotta talk my wife into it," sighed the guy in the DIY center to a mountain-guide-looking woman who was measuring screws.

"Aren't we retired yet?" she replied.

The young guy in Rite Aid said to his friend, "They've cut my hours twice."

A woman advised her husband to "get as many hours as you can."

I was struck again by the contrast between the locals and the visitors when I was biking home and encountered a group of golfers who were crossing the bike path in their golf cart. They were all identically dressed in bright shorts, polo shirts, and visors. They did not say "hi."

Julian reported that the school had an assembly to go over the rules that was so boring that one kid fell asleep. There is a rule against displays of affection. No hand holding, and hugs can be only one second long; Tom and I practiced, and that is very fast—more like chest bumping than hugging. Also, if you have gum, it means automatic detention. *What is it with people's hysteria about gum?* First my niece's babysitter and now Mammoth schools. I'm wondering if they've misinterpreted some state guideline which outlawed any "gun." Julian says gum was a "big problem" at Del Mar Heights because kids stuck it under the desks. "Why not outlaw *that*?" I said.

Also, you're not allowed to wear sports jerseys to school because "it causes fighting." I recall that there was fighting at my junior high school, Central High. Sometimes even girls fought which I found quite shocking. I was amazed that they even knew *how* to fight (more hair pulling, less punching). Tom doesn't remember about his school, and my older son, Luc, doesn't think there was fighting at his school down south. "They fought over grades," he said.

Saturday
It looks as though we have successfully driven off our first neighbors. They brought in an enormous U-Haul truck last night that was gone this morning. They left behind a couch that disappeared a few hours later. I wasn't sad to see them go since their dogs were yappy and they had had a yelling argument on the front porch in front of their small child.

It was my idea to head straight down to the skate park on our bikes for the 16th Annual Wave Rave Skate Contest with a thermos of coffee and eat breakfast while we checked out the scene. It was also my idea to stop by the Shady Rest Park to see if we could get some Little League intelligence. There we discovered a dad hitting fly balls to his young son. They had ridden there on their bikes and brought their dog. It all looked very promising; just as I approached, however, the dog and boy collided in the air as they both went for the ball, resulting in the boy collapsing to the ground in tears. The dad then proceeded to discipline the dog by choking it—which seemed pretty creepy. I did persevere in asking questions between the yelps and tears. He was delighted to talk about Little League and said he was an assistant coach. Upon learning how old Julian is and that he's a catcher, he was even more enthusiastic. "They're looking for twelve-year-olds," he said. "They'll definitely want him. Soccer is just starting too if he's interested in that. I think the teams are already set, but they'll probably let him in. They'll have to, right? I mean, if you've just moved here…" The idea that you wouldn't have to fight your way onto a youth sports team was novel.

It was *not* my idea to pedal all the way up Main Street to Minaret, clamber around to the shuttle stop, take the shuttle all the way up to the Twin Lakes parking lot, and ride around Horseshoe Lake and back down to more off-road trails through Voodoo Chute. We got back about two o'clock, and I collapsed on the couch. "Dad tried to kill us," I told Luc.

He barely looked up from his computer. "Huh," he said.

A few moments later, however, I was inspired to take a bunch of stuff to the Cast Off, the thrift store, to clear things out. Julian's teachers had provided lists of required school supplies and indicated that they could be bought at Rite Aid or Vons. But Rite Aid was a mess with random supplies picked over and scattered around, and no lined paper could be found at all. I struck gold at the Cast Off when I found some lined paper and dividers stuck inside some used binders. The nice ladies at the counter let me buy the innards for eighty-five cents. Living in a remote area will make us more resourceful.

STRANGE EARTH THINGS

Remember, whatever your route, there's no wrong path up 395.

~ JEFF BAKER, BOOKLET ON MAMMOTH LAKES

ONE OF THE most interesting road trips in California is the 120-mile drive along US 395 starting at its intersection with SR 14 near Inyokern and following it up to Carson City, Nevada. Along your drive, geology is brought to life as peculiar rock formations, weird granite spires, dry lakes, perfect cones, sudden crevices, and black lava make an appearance. The landscape, what author Martin Forstenzer calls the "sheer primordial outlandishness of the terrain," leaves the lay person wondering what the heck happened.

If you like desert scenery and really ugly towns, your tour can start earlier at the foot of US 395 in Hesperia, where it heads north from I-15. As you travel through Adelanto and the Victorville area, you enter the Mojave Desert, characterized by endless sage brush, air force bases, and solar panels. It is home to the peculiar Joshua tree, so-called because its upward-reaching branches reminded early Mormon travelers of the biblical story of Joshua raising his arms to the sky. It's a member of the yucca family, and a deep root system supports its thick, heavy branches that end in porcupine-like clumps of spiky leaves. Some specimens can live one thousand years. Gradually, the stretches between towns lengthen, and US 395 joins SR 14 traveling east from Los Angeles and Mojave. Then things get really wild.

∽

The drive is remarkable for the variety of geologic features easily seen from the highway: granite peaks, cinder cones, lava chunks, craters, tombstone rocks, cirque glaciers, and steaming fumaroles. And outside of your car, the entire Eastern Sierra contains dozens of sites worth visiting. Some are truly amazing, like the Devils Postpile, a lava flow that cracked into a towering pile of five- and six-sided columnar rods, or Fossil Falls, where you will find neither fossils nor falls but dry black gouged chutes formed when melting glacial water bored circular potholes into the lava bedrock and fabricated a maze of tunnels and pipes. Others are awesome because of their size, like Obsidian Dome, an unbelievably high pile of sharp shiny broken pieces of volcanic glass. Still others are fitting for quake country, like the Hilton Creek fault scarp in McGee Canyon or the Earthquake Fault or fissure, where an alarming deep crack opened up in the earth's surface, perhaps related to the creation of the Inyo Craters. Those craters were formed when groundwater interacted with magma and exploded to the surface as steam and then cooled to produce the craters' unnaturally yellow and blue waters.

Other sites exhibit different shades of beauty, mysterious or joyful. Mono Lake is simply bizarre with its strangely shaped white tufa towers, created when carbonate-laden fresh water springs entered the alkaline lake. Rock Creek, an artist's delight, is heartbreakingly picturesque, boasting wildflowers and a string of little blue lakes in basins carved out by glaciers. The steaming natural hot springs are fun and remind visitors that they are sharing a tradition with past peoples. And wondrous eye candy continues to emerge, like the 20-foot tall columns of Bishop Tuff at Crowley Lake exposed by receding reservoir water during the recent drought.

The myriad things to look at over the long drive are in part due to the power and number of geologic events that have taken place in the region. As its authors explain in *Geology Underfoot in Death Valley and Owens Valley*, major episodes of volcanism, deposition of thousands of feet of sedimentary rocks, periods of tectonic activity, and several ice-age glaciations provide the ingredients for what they call a "geologic delicacy" or what a French visitor described to me as "strange earth things." There's much to choose from, but let's start with the Sierra Nevada, that imposing mountain range you may have noticed on your left.

∾

The range runs generally north and south along the eastern boundary of the state on the Nevada border. It is three-hundred-fifty miles long and forty to eighty miles wide. From the north, the highest peak barely reaches 8,000 feet. Proceeding south, its summits gradually increase in elevation, with 10,000-foot peaks near Lake Tahoe, 11,000-foot peaks at Sonora Pass, 13,000-foot summits arising in

Yosemite, and our first 14,000-footer in the Palisades, two-hundred-fifty miles south of the north end of the range. There are eleven peaks at 14,000-feet high or higher in the Palisades and around Mount Whitney, the highest mountain in the continental United States at 14,500 feet. The vertical relief here is immense as the basin floor sits at about 4,000 feet, and the mountain range rises two miles up into the sky. It is so high that the sun sets earlier in Lone Pine than in Los Angeles. Mount Langley, the last of the 14,000-foot mountains, lies six miles south of Mount Whitney. From there, the peaks rapidly decrease in elevation, and the Sierra Nevada ends near the Mojave Desert.

The range is enormous, covering an area larger than all of the European Alps put together. The establishment of three national parks in the range—Yosemite, Sequoia, and Kings Canyon—is testimony to the quality and variety of the landscapes found within its environs. Each year, millions of tourists come to see what nature has wrought, and recent years have brought so many travelers that congestion, both on the roads and on the trails, has become a major concern. As the curious stare around at the majestic beauty of the mountains, they surely wonder when and how these phenomenal wonders were created.

⌐ ⌐

Geologist Mary Hill writes that geology is different from other sciences because there is no way to conduct experiments and obtain repeatable results; phenomena that occured during an ice age or while tectonic plates shifted can't be re-created on the same scale in a laboratory. Instead, the study of geology requires the interpretation of what exists today to unfurl the mystery of what came before. In the Sierra Nevada it's a tale of fire and ice, forces beyond our imagination, intractable slow motion over millions of years interspersed by brief violent dramatic events, a story still being unraveled by scientists today.

The range's current still, cold, icy appearance belies the heat, fire, and convulsion that launched our rousing story. It took over 100 million years to create the batholith, meaning "deep rock," the gigantic granite block that we know of as the backbone of the Sierra Nevada. Over 200 million years ago, deep underground, molten rock began to cool, forming granite and rising toward the surface. This granite block gave us the overall shape of the range, but, over the next 100 million years, its response to other factors—rain, wind, ice, and water—is what carved the beauty into the rock. Granite rock breaks in two major ways: along joints that are even up-and-down planes, or horizontally in sheets where it breaks along a curved line parallel to the surface of the rock. Joint breaks produce the sharp, steep faces of the Sierra while sheeting produces the dome features so prevalent in Yosemite.

At that time, an enormous sea covered the area, and the "young" granite block pushed up the sedimentary rock that had lain on the bottom of the sea. The old sedimentary rock can be seen where it was shoved aside in the foothills or seen in the high Sierra as roof pendants, sometimes called rock hats. Paleozoic rock, dating from 450 million years ago, is found in the Mount Morrison area at Convict Lake and is nearly the oldest rock in the Sierra. Its life of gathering sediments for millions of years under water is portrayed by its beautiful orange, brown, and white layers. Even Mammoth Rock, which looks like granite, is actually marble and also predates the formation of the Sierra Nevada. It once sat on the western edge of Pangaea, the supercontinent that bordered the sea, so if you put your mind back 300 million years, you can imagine waves lapping at its feet.

The junctures between granite and old rock stimulated mineralization, which sounds pretty boring until you realize I'm talking about gold and silver, treasures that are abundant in the Sierra compared to the rest of the earth. Minerals formed deep beneath the surface 150 million years ago found a way to rise to the surface during the time of earthquakes by traveling along fault lines. On the west side of the Sierra, gold would be discovered in thin wandering sheets of quartz called veins that marked an ancient crack where the earth had slipped against itself. On the east side, gold was more finely disseminated, and, without the benefit of the veins, ore had to be laboriously crushed to extract what small amounts of gold had formed.

Besides quartz, other minerals such as feldspar, mica, amphibole, and calcite are found in the Sierra along with various gems and significant amounts of tungsten. This has led to a lot of modern day frenetic digging, blasting, picking, hosing, sluicing, crushing, dredging, and sifting in the Sierra over the past 150 years. Most of the activity, especially the environmentally disastrous hydraulic mining, took place, however, on the western slopes of the Sierra.

The periods of uplift of the giant granite block continued for millions of years during the Tertiary period, when the Alps and the Himalayas were also rising. The final significant uplift occurred about three million years ago, raising the east side some 6,000 feet, although those rising forces are still at work today. The mountain range eventually tilted toward the west, resulting in the precipitous eastern side while the western slope rises gradually to the crest over many miles. The range's height and rugged eastern escarpment would be further emphasized when the Great Basin on the east side of the Sierra fell, adding another 500 feet to the vertical relief.

As if that weren't exciting enough, about thirty million years ago, volcanoes began to erupt along the range, spewing blankets of hot ash and volcanic mud flows over the northern Sierra. When the mountain range underwent its final uplift, it was accompanied by powerful earthquakes and other mayhem. This activity is characteristic of the "ring of fire," a horseshoe-shaped zone of intense volcanic activity around the Pacific Ocean. More than 75 percent of the world's active or dormant volcanoes lie in this region, and over 90 percent of the earth's earthquakes occur here. Californians are well aware of ongoing earthquake activity as hardly a decade goes by without a significant earthquake in the state, and cracked sidewalks and foundations provide a visual reminder of the constant movement along our faults.

∽

After undergoing colossal changes due to forces under its surface, the Sierra was then pounded by elements from above as the icy fingers of snow and glaciers would sculpt the breathtaking peaks and valleys on view today. A glacier begins with a snowflake, what John Muir called "a tender snow-flower, the offspring of the sun and sea," whose light weight and delicate shape change into the powerful blue ice of a glacier through a series of transformations. The snowflake usually starts as a hexagonal crystal and attaches itself to other snowflakes after falling from the sky. As the snowflakes bind more and more tightly and are compressed under more snow, they recrystallize excluding air to form an ice mass gaining weight and density. It turns into firn after a few years and a firm glacier after many years, made up of crystals of glacial ice that can reach ten inches in length.

A glacier's ability to flow under the pressure of its own mass and to gather rocks and sand as scouring tools make it a powerful agent of erosion. Unlike river-carved V-shaped canyons, glacier-formed canyons are typically U-shaped, as tremendous rocks carried by the glacier grind and scrape the sides of the valley and smaller rocks act like sandpaper to shine and polish the sides and bottom. That phenomenon gave rise to the glossy striated appearance of so much of our granite in the Eastern Sierra.

When a glacier retreats, it leaves behind stark ridges and sharp peaks, also called matterhorns, and spoon-shaped hollows, known as cirques. These depressions are formed behind moraines, ridges of rocks and sand that the glacier had been carrying and dropped when it stopped moving. Tarn lakes often are left behind in cirques, and a series of lakes stepping down the mountainside may be connected by waterfalls. John Muir called all this work "exceptional destruction."

Yosemite Valley, the centerpiece of Yosemite National Park, is a textbook example of glacial erosion illustrated by its domes and peaks, steep cliffs, awe-inspiring waterfalls, and lush meadows on the broad valley floor. In the words of Francis Farquhar, a famous Sierra Club president, Yosemite Valley's discovery by white people "would mark the beginning of a century of descriptions that practically exhausted the thesaurus of adjectives." Hetch Hetchy Valley, also located in Yosemite National Park, was arguably as spectacular until it was filled up with water to become a giant reservoir for thirsty San Franciscans, a project that the Sierra Club and John Muir fought but failed to stop.

Looking at the larger picture, "ice age" turns out not to be a useful term because we have various cooling and warming trends inside longer cold periods, and our long-lived Earth may be in the middle of an ongoing ice age that goes back two million years. Definitions and boundaries of these cold periods continue to be refined, but the main factor in climate patterns appears to be variations in the Earth's orbit, called Milankovitch cycles. We do know that the Sierra experienced three significant cold pulses, the Tahoe, the Tenaya, and—the most recent—the Tioga, whose evidence is everywhere, especially in our moraines and cirques. The Tahoe was the most severe; at its height seventy thousand years ago, glaciers probably covered three hundred miles along the crest, shoving long tongues down into the canyons toward the foothills.

The Tioga was part of the Wisconsin glaciation, the last major advance of glaciers in North America. It created the Great Lakes, radically altered the geography of the continent, and, at its glacial maxima, permitted the migration of mammals—including people—to the New World. In my home state of Indiana, glaciers had an obvious effect on the landscape; they flattened the northern half of the state but retreated before they reached the hills and forests of Southern Indiana. The melting glaciers also created Southern Indiana's karst topography by burrowing into the limestone bedrock, leaving behind our mysterious sink holes and caves.

A local contrast in glaciation can be seen in the rounded Alabama Hills, untouched by glaciers, but severely weathered and eroded by the corrosive action of chemicals carried by rainwater and by water freezing and expanding in cracks in the rocks. In comparison, above loom the craggy peaks of the Sierra Nevada, the work of long-gone glaciers. A few glaciers still exist in the Sierra, like the Palisades Glacier, but they are descendants of a modern glaciation that reached its height in the eighteenth century. Like glaciers around the world, they have been shrinking or disappearing in the face of sharp increases in the earth's surface temperature since 1980.

US 395 goes straight up the middle of Owens Valley, a long narrow trough running north and south, bounded by fault lines that lie at the base of the Sierra Nevada and the Inyo Mountains, the two ranges that hem in the valley. Basins such as these are characteristic of the Basin and Range Province and result from the stretching of the earth's crust as the North American Plate on which it sits pulls away from the Pacific Plate. Owens Valley is the westernmost basin or graben (German for "ditch") of this province.

Sights in Owens Valley provide clues as to the transformations the land has undergone in the recent past—at least recent from a geological standpoint—during the last couple hundred years or so. When the ghosts of former lakes appear, white and shimmering in the distance, we are reminded of the California Water Wars in which Owens Valley played such a significant role. A rusty water tower sits abandoned near a large sign that commands, "Take Care of the Sierras." If it's been put there by the Los Angeles Department of Water and Power, it is the ironic equivalent of an enthusiastic do-gooder who puts a Sierra Club sticker on his gas-guzzling SUV. Little rain falls in the valley, but its present-day aridity is the result of the aqueducts built by the Los Angeles Department of Water and Power that whisk away the tremendous waters flowing out of the Sierra in the summer.

The sign also offends by using the vilified plural "Sierras" which Ansel Adams said was a "linguistic, Californian, and mountaineering sin." Let me see if I can explain why people get so freaked out about the pluralization. The Sierra Nevada was named by some Spanish explorers who caught sight of the range in the distance. Because it was covered with snow, they named it "Sierra" for "mountain range" and "Nevada" for "snowy." "Sierra," which also means "saw blade," was a word for a mountain range because the silhouette of the mountain peaks resembles the teeth of a saw blade. So, you would not say, "I'm going to the Sawblades today"; that would be confusing and imply that you were going to multiple mountain ranges. You would say, "I'm going to the Sawblade today" or, more poetically, "I'm going to the Sierra." Hope that helps.

As you look east across Owens Valley, you see the White Mountains that take over to form the eastern wall of the valley once the Inyo Mountains peter out around Big Pine. The name Inyo comes from a Native American word meaning the dwelling place of the Great Spirit. The White Mountains are nearly as high as the Sierra Nevada but are quite different, being much older and more arid. They are formed of Paleozoic rock, about six hundred million years old.

Almost nothing can grow in the White Mountains because of the dry, cold climate, banks of dusty dolomite soil, and constant wind. One thing does like to grow there: the bristlecone pine, which has enjoyed the lack of competition for thousands of years. The Ancient Bristlecone Pine Forest in the White Mountains contains numerous trees over four thousand years old, by far the oldest of any plant or animal species on Earth. For comparison, the old giant sequoias, those massive trees that grow to be three hundred feet tall, are a thousand years younger—merely middle-aged compared to these elders.

An amusing side note about the sequoias is the argument over their name that took place back in 1854. At a botanist meeting in France, the name *Sequoia gigantea* was proposed based on its similarity to the Coast Redwood, or *Sequoia sempervirens*. A politically-minded English botanist proposed that the tree be named *Sequoia wellingtonia* after the Duke of Wellington. Then the Americans turned patriotic and proposed that it be named *Sequoia washingtoniana*. After a big fight, most manuals now refer to *Sequoia gigantea*, although I notice the Park Service refers to *Sequoia washingtoniana*. Then in 1939, another botanist said they were all wrong, and it should be *Sequoiadendron*, not Sequoia. Although not adopted by laypeople, or even many botanists, Wikipedia's entry does indeed refer to the mouthful *Sequoiadendron giganteum*.

∽

If you are like thousands of Southern Californians who make the drive up US 395, your journey will end at Mammoth Mountain, the world-class ski resort known for its deep snow and sunny skies. The mountain is actually a volcano, and a fairly young one at that, produced by multiple eruptions between 50,000 and 150,000 years ago. They resulted in what US Geological Survey scientist Wes Hildreth calls a "late Pleistocene pile of silicic lava domes." Say that three times fast. It was originally called Pumice Mountain for its expanses of the crumbly light-colored rock that commonly forms in silicic lavas. Pumice is astonishingly light and can initially float in water, to the amusement of kids on field trips. Mammoth Mountain is more than four miles wide from east to west and at 11,053 feet is the highest ski resort in California.

It experienced a steam eruption seven hundred years ago, and its fumaroles continue to spew poisonous gases. One fumarole inside the ski area was responsible for the suffocation deaths of several ski patrol members in 2006, and a large carbon dioxide discharge on its southern flank, near Horseshoe Lake, has killed trees in a 170-acre area. Measurements and chemical analysis of the emissions indicate that the mountain is releasing twelve hundred tons of carbon dioxide every day, somewhat in conflict with the community's reputation as a green town. Furthermore, it appears that there is a large reservoir of gas deep inside the mountain that is escaping to the surface along fault lines. It's easy to forget when you're flying down Broadway headed for an après-ski drink that the slopes beneath your skis belong to a volcano, now defined as extinct, but still capable of last-gasp outbursts.

~

While you're in Mammoth, you might want to snowshoe up to my favorite spot, Minaret Vista, which offers its own interesting perspective on geologic artifacts. As you stand at the summit, you can look down at the wide river gorge, first incised by rushing water and then scrubbed out by glaciers. You can also look across at the mysterious Minarets, whose dark angular spires have weathered so differently from other Sierra peaks, giving rise to their sensational appearance and taunting challenge to rock climbers.

Less visible is that you are standing on a watershed anomaly, a disparity between the drainage divide and the crestal divide. On one side of you, snowmelt flows into the San Joaquin River and off to the Pacific; on the other, it flows into the Owens River and is diverted to faucets in Los Angeles. What is peculiar is that you are looking across the river at the Ritter Range, the crest of the Sierra, which is *west* of you. So how did the headwaters of the San Joaquin end up on the other side of the Sierra crest? Answer: geology.

Before the Sierra experienced its great rise, the San Joaquin's watershed area probably extended as far east as Nevada. As the mountains began to rise, the river found that its way westward was barred by the impenetrable Ritter Range, made of Mesozoic volcanic rock. That rock is over one hundred million years old (imagine—the age of dinosaurs!) and much harder than granite. Seeking an easier pathway, the river turned until it could find an opening through softer rock at the southern end of the range. Our section of the San Joaquin, the so-called Middle Fork, runs north and south, which is unusual for most rivers in California, particularly those in the Sierra.

Eventually the river channel north of us was blocked by lava flows, and the Middle Fork was cut off from the east. It now finds some of its headwaters at Thousand Island Lake, that spectacular pristine alpine tarn made famous by Ansel Adams' photos. It's a shame that not everyone gets to see Thousand Island Lake; it might make us more sensitive to the state of our rivers and how we use water in California. Because of excessive damming and diversions, the American Rivers organization identified the San Joaquin as the most endangered river in the nation for 2014 and ranked it second for 2016.

⌒〜

The Eastern Sierra is constantly being reworked by erosion, wind, avalanches, rock slides, and human activity. However it is also geologically still in its youth, a dynamic region on the move, while invisible forces work under its surface. Earthquakes continue to the current day, a reminder that things are only comparatively quieter now. In 1872, which is about a fraction of a second ago in geological time, a massive earthquake, one of the largest ever to hit California, struck the town of Lone Pine, collapsing buildings and killing twenty-seven people. Although no modern world seismographs existed in 1872, scientists have since estimated the Lone Pine quake to have been near an 8.0 magnitude, on par with the great 1906 quake in San Francisco. In Lone Pine, a twelve-mile-long crack in the land opened up, shocking the residents who did not have the benefit of a geologist nearby to explain that this was all to be expected. The crack is visible from US 395 on your left as you drive north out of Lone Pine. If you look carefully (assuming you're not driving), you might be able to follow it for ten miles out of town.

Currents deep in the earth's mantle continue to cause the giant tectonic plates that form its crust to shift and rise and bang into each other, wreaking havoc on the surface. California sits on two of the most active plates, the Pacific and North American Plates, which are moving about as fast as your fingernails grow. Where these two plates slide past each other, they create faults like the San Andreas fault, but where they pull apart, they stretch the crust into a basin, such as Owens Valley. This activity, called tectonism, produces faults, earthquakes, and volcanoes, just the stuff our home is known for.

One of the most spectacular of these occurred relatively recently, 760,000 years ago. Long Valley, near Mammoth Mountain in northern Owens Valley, was the site of a colossal eruption when magma exploded from a set of vents in the valley and threw out 150 cubic miles of volcanic debris. The blast was two thousand times greater than the eruption of Mount St. Helens, sending ash twenty-five miles in the air so violently that it has been found in Nebraska and Kansas. The resulting depression was two miles deep, but most of the material fell straight back to earth, filling up two-thirds of the hole, which then collapsed, leaving a ten- by twenty-mile volcanic field called the Long Valley Caldera. Only one preexisting mountain survives: Glass Mountain, made of obsidian that formed when magma leaked from the caldera before it exploded.

Filled with thousands of feet of solidified ash, the basin contains the pinkish rock known as Bishop Tuff, which today can confound well drillers by spewing hot pink silt onto their neighbors' lawns. The rock is also a geological movie star and made an appearance in *Tremors* when one of the movie's monsters emerged from its surface. Much of our understanding of this area is thanks to Roy Bailey, a scientist with the US Geological Survey, who dedicated a significant portion of his career to the study of the caldera. Bailey was known for his meticulous observations and beautiful maps. In the seventies, he built on the work of Charles Gilbert, a geologist at the University of California, Berkeley, and alum of Deep Springs College, who had determined the origin of the tuff.

Even more recently in May of 1980, only the blink of an eye ago, four earthquakes of 6.0 magnitudes occurred in the caldera, just north of Convict Lake. Scientists had observed that the caldera had developed a mysterious bulge in the area over the previous few years, but they had not anticipated the big quakes. They caused tremendous rock slides, huge boulders were flung down into the McGee Creek pack station corrals, and an exceptionally large boulder fell down a slope north of the airport. That monstrosity measured over twenty feet across and left craters six feet deep behind as it bounced down the hill, astonishing a group of geology students from the University of California, Santa Cruz, who happened to be on site for a field trip. Takeaway lesson from the field trip? Look uphill during an earthquake so you can dodge the boulders crashing down on you.

It was thought at the time that the quakes were probably caused by the intrusion of a dike, a thin tabular mass of magma, rather than by rocks moving along a fault. Such a dike near SR 203, the only way out of town, raised concerns that townspeople would be trapped if the road were blocked. Town officials hurriedly built another section of road further north from SR 203 out to US 395; they wisely decided to call it the Mammoth Scenic Loop, instead of the "Mammoth Escape Route," to the relief of real estate agents.

To further investigate the dike, the US Geological Survey lowered instruments into Resurgent Dome (a bump raised by magma) nearly down to sea level to study the movements and temperature of magma down where there is no interference from surface noise. The discovery that it was cold down to seven thousand feet reassured scientists that an imminent eruption was unlikely. In fact, University of California, Berkeley, geologist Bob Drake told me that now it's more likely something would happen near the Inyo Craters since they are much younger. Ironically, they are located along the Scenic Loop.

Volcanism has shaped our local landscape for 3.5 million years, and gas emissions and earthquakes, including three 5.5+ magnitude earthquakes in December 2016, indicate our region is still very active. Scientists continue to focus on this area to study earthquakes, dikes, and magma. Carleton College also uses Mammoth Lakes for educational purposes; in a role-playing scenario called "The Sleeping

Mountain," the townspeople are told the risks of a volcanic eruption and must debate whether or not to abandon the town. The course materials point out that none of the tourist websites mention the volcanoes. As for the locals and me, we've decided to stay. Surrounded by young volcanoes, we can't predict when the next "big one" will come, nor how big it will be, only that it will. Intrigued and resigned, we live with the odds.

∽

There's still lots to see as you continue north on US 395. The Sierra is immense and worth exploring throughout because of its infinite variety. Paul Webster wrote in *The Mighty Sierra*, "The Sierra changes its features yet retains its identity; each valley, each meadow, each crag is something like all the others, yet in some way different."

I enjoy imagining what our region looked like when humans first came here. It is remarkable to look at old photographs and see how little has changed, so different from the major transformations that have taken place elsewhere in California. In coastal Southern California, so much earthmoving has taken place that only major land features remain. It's hard to believe that California was settled less than 200 years ago, and that 250 years ago the only towns were small Spanish outposts. When I look at our comparatively pristine views, I like to daydream about what thoughts young Native Americans might have had or what worries occupied their minds when they looked at our Eastern Sierra landscape. The land brings a close connection to our companions, locally close, but temporally far away.

The cliffs around June Lake are exceptionally lovely, Mono Lake is a must see, and you can join the millions who each year visit

Yosemite to gape at its endless beauty. The beaver ponds at Lundy Canyon, the mining ghost town of Bodie, the bird-watchers' paradise at Topaz Lake, the old mint in Carson City, the thirty-mile stretch where the West Walker River washed out the highway after a big snow year, and more are waiting for you. Just watch out for deer.

Illustration – The Mammoth Lakes Post Office

YELLOW CARDS AND OTHER LOCAL COLOR

Hey, moron, grow a pair!

~ NOTE ON FLYER AT THE POST OFFICE

A VISIT TO the Mammoth Lakes post office in the summertime is worth the trip even if you don't get any mail to throw away. The building's workaday exterior is glamorized by bountiful flower gardens, and more subtle surprises await to be discovered inside. The local color can be hidden in Mammoth unless you know where to look. The post office is such a place, like a crack in the picture, a portal you can slip through and find yourself in a different—perhaps not universe—but a different experience than most have when they come to town to ski.

It was a lovely August day when my husband, Tom, and I decided to address the issue of receiving mail locally now that we were living here full time. The USPS doesn't deliver mail to residences in town, so locals have to obtain a PO Box. Some municipalities have chosen this option to encourage community building by requiring everyone to visit their post office. That is not the case in Mammoth Lakes; here it's because of the logistical problems posed by regular, heavy snow.

You don't necessarily have to pay for your PO Box; if you can prove you have a local residence, you can get one for free. Our extended family had had a PO Box years ago, but its upkeep and fees had become the responsibility of no one, so it had faded into obscurity along with vague memories of late notices and missing keys. We were ready for a fresh start but braced for considerable bureaucracy, as seems to be the wont of most USPS offices. We went in with low expectations, reminding each other that we lacked necessary documentation to actually obtain a box and that this was just a reconnaissance run.

We held the door for a woman who came out looking pleased, with a package from Amazon tucked under her arm. As I entered the building, another woman standing at the end of the corridor had unwrapped her package and, looking inside, did a little jig. When she caught sight of me, she stopped jigging. "Sorry," she said, but she still looked pretty happy. It turns out that Mammoth has a tradition of dancing when the mail comes in.

∽

Mail delivery in Mono County has a romantic history. In the olden days, mail was delivered to the local mining towns by ski, mule, and even dogsled teams in a big sack by anybody heading up to Mammoth from Bishop. Beginning in 1923, when the town was but a tiny camp beside Mammoth Creek, mail was delivered daily to the general store run by Lloyd and Sybil Summers. They installed a window with a shelf and sorted the mail into cubbyholes in a corner of the store. It wasn't an official post office, but it was a start. Back then, the camp was just known as "Mammoth." Historical photographs picture it as a disorderly line of wooden buildings, including a barn, rooming house, two hotels, and the general store with a hand pump for gasoline on its porch.

When SR 203 was built in 1937 and the town picked up and relocated alongside the new thoroughfare, Tex Cushion's sled dogs would bring the mail in winter from the patrol station in what was soon to be called "Old Mammoth" over to Penney's Tavern next to the new highway. The locals would gather in front of the big fireplace in the late afternoon to rummage through the mail spread out on a table and perhaps stay to party into the evening, drinking and dancing.

Frequent entertainment at the tavern in those days was provided by Walter "Sage" McKinney and Sons, an old-time string band. Walter was a steel guitarist who played with the Tennessee Ramblers until he took the notion to move to California. I easily imagine the hardworking locals back then staying warm on a chilly evening with a circle dance or a little western swing. The real question is: If a hot band set up in the post office parking lot on a Saturday morning today, would the locals pause on their errands to show off a move or two?

In 1941, the town successfully petitioned Congress for regular mail delivery from Bishop six days a week. After it turned out that the name Mammoth was already taken by a community in far Northern California, the town became Mammoth Lakes. With the town's step-up in legitimacy, the Summers family moved a small cabin from their pack station to the south side of the highway and installed the mail boxes from the general store. Sybil Summers became known as the "smiling postmistress," as she fulfilled her duties cheerfully, except the day when her car skidded off the road and flipped over several times while she was driving to work. In true Mammoth fashion, she crawled out, made it up to the road, and hailed a ride down to the post office where shortly thereafter she was sorting mail, just a little bruised and battered.

Sybil and the post office moved across the street in 1948, near the post office's current location, into fancy new digs in a stone building that also housed the K and L ice store, which offered quick freezing, deer storage, cold lockers, and fish packing and shipping. Meanwhile the busy little pack station cabin was moved back to the pack station near Lake Mary to become a bunkhouse. The large stone building was demolished in 1965 and the post office was moved to a new small red lodge on the post office's current lot, along with a bank.

The town was growing quickly between 1965 and 1985, and a second post office was opened among some store fronts on Old Mammoth Road near Sherwin Plaza to accommodate the growing population. PO Boxes were so hard to come by that many residents had to stand in line for USPS General Delivery. When the current post office opened in 1985, the second post office closed.

Now over thirty years old, the post office is a chunky structure, clad in somber gray siding, set stolidly back from Main Street, like an austere, elderly aunt at a bachelorette party. If you could build a post office in Minecraft, this is what it would look like: symmetrical cubes pasted together covered by a flat roof, seemingly unsuited for an alpine climate. Inside, it resembles a small airport with an expanse of skylights overlooking two long halls bordered by windows. The wide, sunny hallways lead the visitor to the thousands of PO Boxes that service the local population, those who live here year-round and those who own second homes here.

On the outside, the wildflower gardens in front and along the side are resplendent with lilies, poppies, monkey flowers, buttercups—an unapologetic tableau of tall purple, blue, yellow, and white blossoms.

It's as though someone threw out several handfuls of wildflower seed and nature said, "Thanks. I'll take it from here," and decided to illustrate just how much it could wow you. The eye-popping result can last all the way into October.

The side entrance into the post office has been modified to install two access ramps. Because the ramps' railings now block direct access to the closest door, many people use a door further down the building. Or you can do what many locals do. Although I wasn't surprised to see thirteen-year-old free-skier Sean vault the railing on his way in and out, I was a little astonished to see several grownups do the same, including a guy who was definitely past his spring-chicken phase and a middle-aged woman who carefully climbed over the railing. People who live in Mammoth Lakes don't shy away from a little physical exertion.

The post office is where you may encounter the unique nature of Mammoth Lakes residents, a gruff, interested, in-your-face friendliness—a mixture of Crocodile Dundee, the Bronx, and a bear. "See anything good?" a man roared one day when he spied me reading the bulletin board. There's usually something good on the bulletin board, if not directly useful like an ad for the perfect used snowboard or an announcement of an interesting concert, then certainly informative from an anthropological standpoint, like the woman who advertised for a room or "just a place to camp that's safe." Or the advertisement for a chain-saw-sharpening service: "Don't go into Devils Postpile with a dull blade." Or the poster for "Families of Problem Drinkers" that invites you to "come share what we have in common."

On this day, I definitely saw something good—the Booky Joint had posted a "Help Wanted" sign that said, "Must like to read." *Are you kidding me? A job at the marvelous, colorful bookstore full of sur-*

prises and Lego? With some trepidation, I decided to apply in person the next day.

The next day, however, when I stopped once again by the post office, the sign was *gone. What did that mean? Had the job been filled in twenty-four hours?* When I asked hesitantly at the bookstore if the position was still open, the owner told me he was well aware that the sign had been taken down. He said that by scrutinizing the applications he had received so far, he was trying to figure out who had done it.

"I have a suspect," he said.

Removing notices for competitive reasons was apparently not uncommon as I learned when I read this scribbled note on a flyer advertising firewood: "Hey, moron, why don't you man up and give me a call and we can talk about this. Don't take this notice down again! Grow a pair!" The wording of and sentiment behind this text is so quintessentially Mammoth Lakes that it should be memorialized on a T-shirt.

Reading the bulletin board can offer other insights into the community and its inhabitants. One man advertised his services as a "General Laborer" and included a photo, presumably of himself, showing a burly, bearded, pony-tailed man cutting up a huge tree with a very long handsaw. A woman advertised for a vegetarian roommate, and although she described herself as easy going, she requested that the roommate "have similar values and be accountable." Her values were self-reported as "generally liberal spiritual values and view-points." She wrote that "male or female and age doesn't matter—much." If you "fit the bill," you could write or email.

Some people try to help the posters. One elaborate flyer about a car for sale included considerable detail, including the age of the battery and Bluetooth capability, but some critical information was missing, as pointed out by someone who scrawled on the ad: "WHAT is iT!!!!" and someone else added more gently, "What year is it?"

~

Meanwhile, back at the postal counter, a thoughtful man (later identified as the spouse of a future colleague of mine at the town offices) listened carefully to our story, which came out a bit garbled and sounded highly suspicious, even to me, as though we were fraudulently trying to get a free PO Box.

"We're just trying to find out what we need to bring in," my husband said, a bit wildly.

The man pursed his lips and looked at us gravely. "It looks as though you have some documentation right there," he said, gesturing to the utility bill Tom was clutching.

"Well, I don't know if this is good enough. And I only have one," Tom protested, but the man took the bill, smoothed it out, and looked it over.

"This is fine," he said. "Now I just need some identification that has your name on it. It could be a car registration, a..."

"Car registration! We have that!" I said excitedly. Tom dashed out to the car while I stepped out of line. My eye fell on a collection of keys hanging at one of the counters, and I felt immediately guilty.

~

On a school morning bike ride, Tom and I came across a set of keys lying in the road. Anxious to demonstrate our level of good citizenship to the community, we picked them up and took them home, intent on finding their owner. I puzzled over them for an hour, looking for clues about who they belonged to, Googling the words on the key chain and the numbers engraved on the keys. Nuttin'. So we wrote up two big signs and posted one on a tree near where the keys were dropped and another at the post office. I waited anxiously by the phone, worrying about the dismay of the owner when he discovered his keys were missing. Going even a day without one's keys could be a big problem. Tom encouraged me to get on with my life.

Twenty-four hours later, we got a call from Shasta, the keys' owner, and he came by to pick them up. He explained that he had discovered their disappearance just after he dropped them in the street and had turned right around to go back to where he had parked. Although he noticed a couple of bike riders (us), he didn't think to stop us until he got back to the scene of the crime and learned from some bystanders that the bikers had picked up a set of keys. He then whipped back along Majestic Pines to track us down, but by then, we had snuck into our garage and shut the door. I listened to this story with increasing horror. This meant we had actually kept his keys *away from him* for a day. So much for being Good Samaritans. Fortunately, Shasta guffawed at my embarrassment and accepted my apologies.

"We found a set of keys and didn't know how to find the owner," I told Kristen the next day. Kristen's my go-to person for all things local.

"You should have taken them to Chuck," she said. "Remember the guy from the concert?"

I did recall a tall stooped gentleman whom Kristen had pointed out as a postal clerk.

"You'll get to know him," she said confidently. She explained that Chuck had a set of hooks at his station where all the lost keys get lined up and wait for their owners to appear. In fact, Shasta had mentioned that he had checked at the post office for his keys. Sigh. This is what happens when newbies come to town.

☙❧

Through the post office windows, I could see the car registration document that Tom was carrying back from our van. My heart sank. It looked mutilated, with a hole chopped into the middle of it as though it had something to hide. *That rag was supposed to serve as some kind of official document?* I had my doubts. The hole was the work of my husband who has concerns—some would say excessive concerns—about home security. He presented the document with a flourish to the female clerk who had taken over the counter.

"It has a hole in it because..." I started, and then stopped.

"Have you ever seen *Bad Santa?*" Tom asked her abruptly.

"The one with Billy Bob Thornton?" She didn't seem surprised one bit.

"Yes." Tom didn't seem surprised either. "You know how in the movie he broke into a house after he stole a car because the address was on the vehicle registration?"

"Uh-huh," she said, looking very interested. (Later, a defiantly-not-paranoid friend would breathe, "He was *polluting* her.")

"That's why you should cut your address out like this," Tom said confidently.

"That's true," she said, nodding slowly. "I never thought of that."

Did I detect an admiring tone in her voice? That note told me that Tom was going to fit right in. In short order, we had ourselves a PO Box.

A few days later we stopped by the post office to collect our mail and discovered a Netflix movie waiting for us. Now we had really arrived.

∽

At first we were amused to see a dedicated mail slot for Netflix movies, marked "NETFLIX ONLY," but after we had made several dozen trips to the post office ourselves to both pick up and mail back those special red envelopes, it didn't seem odd at all. Similarly, the yellow cards, while initially exotic, became routine.

Most packages are sent to the post office and most of us have small PO Boxes—too small for the typical package. Notification that something is ready for pickup at the counter is communicated by way of a long yellow card marked with your box number and placed in your box. With the volume of stuff arriving into this remote area where mail order is heavily relied on, the cards are used and reused; dozens of numbers can be marked on and crossed off the card. Half the people standing in line at any given moment may be grasping yellow cards. When one person with a yellow card has arrived at the head of the line, the clerks kindly collect cards from everyone and head back into the storage area with a handful of yellow cards. While they retrieve our stuff, we mill around in anticipation.

Nearing Christmas, the number of yellow cards increased significantly. It seemed as though the town was being flooded with packages. The clerk sent a mob of us to a separate distribution window and pulled up a cart so loaded with packages that someone called out, "Ho ho **HO**!" which made us all laugh. I got two boxes that were so enormous I could barely manage them. When their bulk caused me to drop my mail, some nice ladies helped me restack everything, picked up my gloves for me, and held the door open. As I put my boxes in my trunk, a woman walked by and cooed, "Oooo, packages."

Another day, while we yellow-card people were waiting for our packages, the couple next to me was burbling about what might be coming. Two men with canes noticed each other and pointed their accessories aggressively at each other. "Sword fight," one of them chuckled before coming over to talk about the Mayo Clinic. The postal worker came out of the back office clutching a mound of boxes in her arms and holding the pile down with her chin.

"Shutterfly! Oooo," the wife whispered to her husband.

"Ooo-ooo," he said in response, and they almost hopped with excitement.

The Shutterfly book was indeed for them, someone got a huge box from Zappos, and I received a ZipBook, courtesy of a state grant to benefit libraries in remote areas.

The postal clerk held up an unclaimed box. "841?" she queried. No response.

"I'll take it!" a man called out. He had been charming me with an enthusiastic description of some special cooking oil he was anticipating would come any day.

When the clerk just looked harassed instead of amused, the cooking oil guy said to me, "Can't joke around in here. The post office is a serious place." Then he whispered, "Don't want anyone to go *postal*. Although," he continued, nodding at the speaker droning out tinny Christmas tunes, "if I had to listen to that all day, I might go postal." I smiled.

∽

The post office is a place of greeting. Very often while you are there, two people who know each other will meet and exchange information or gossip.

A man and a woman ran into each other in the parking lot, and there was a brief exchange of personal news.

"You just got back into town last night?" the man queried. "How was your drive?"

"Oh, fine," she said. "Long."

"So," he said, putting his foot on the running board of her car and getting down to business. "Have you been watching *True Detective*?"

The post office is also a good place to hear the weather forecast, especially when snow is on the horizon. "I think we'll see snow in the next day or so," a man commented to his friend one day in the hallway.

"That's very intuitive of you," the second guy said and grinned.

"Yeah, it comes with the genes," the first guy retorted. "Or an Internet connection."

Another day, two women were talking to each other when I walked in. I wasn't eavesdropping until one of them burst into tears.

"I'm just ready for the end," she cried.

"You don't mean that," said her friend.

"Oh yes, I do," she said. "I'm having a really hard day today."

They embraced in the middle of all the PO Boxes and said goodbye. A conversation like that can make you think the post office is a pretty important place.

∽

On one of our first days as year-round residents, I followed an old Subaru into the post office parking lot. The car sported an array of bumper stickers, signifying "local" and "a character," and the nose of a motley sheep dog sticking out the back window. As we both climbed the incline leading to the post office building, another car driven by a little old lady slowly drifted across our lane, heading toward the drive-up mail box. An arm emerged from the Subaru, palm facing up, fingers extended in exasperation, just the arm—no honk. The arm turned out to belong to a troll-looking woman who entered the post office before me, checked her PO Box, threw her mail away in the recycling bin, muttering—and then lurched out the door in front of me and heaved herself back into her car. Again, I followed her as we drove back down the rise where once more her path was impeded by a Suburban stopped in the exit lane for no apparent reason. Out came the arm again.

It can be a challenge to exit the post office onto Main Street because of the cross traffic and multiple vehicles entering the driveway. The original plan was for traffic to enter from Main Street and exit out the back, but plans changed, and now the traffic flows awkwardly around the parking lot and back out onto Main. A cautious driver can wait quite a while before a big enough gap opens up to pull out safely. A soccer dad had complained about it to me one day, saying, "You can sit there for ten minutes behind some woman with no balls," which struck me as a less-than-fair criticism of the opposite sex. Today, the troll decided to give it a pass and snuck down the access road to a less busy intersection. Observing her maneuver, I followed her. Ha ha! Local knowledge.

GETTING HIGH

*Mammoth Mountain, the Minarets, Mt. Ritter and
Banner Peak… their looming presence could
care less about Tulsa v. Indiana State.*

~ TIM ALPERS, LONGTIME LOCAL AND COLLEGE
BASKETBALL COACH, *MY SPHERE OF INFLUENCE*

August 24–28, 2014
Sunday

THIS MORNING AFTER a breakfast of waffles and bananas, I sat and
read the paper. I cannot remember the last time I did that—it must
have been sometime around 1993. Then it was off to Fall Ball baseball
where Julian has found his way onto a team. On the way, I picked
up *A Prairie Home Companion* on the Reno radio station. Driving
down US 395, with the mountains shining in the sun and Garrison
Keillor telling his story, Julian beside me in his baseball gear, I got a
burst of euphoria.

Whitmore Recreation Area is located down by the airport, a good
1,000 feet below the town, which helps with snow issues. It is comprised of three baseball fields, one of which is high school regulation
size, and a spectacular running track around an artificial turf soccer

field, as well as a public swimming pool nearby. How those facilities got built in a town that had filed for bankruptcy two years before is an interesting story, but one for another day.

The ball field was *hot*. I neglected to take into account the change in elevation, and it was steaming down there. About forty boys showed up, and the parents were excited about that. They were also excited about the cattle guard that had been installed at the entrance to the park complex. Two mothers explained to me what a hassle it had been to clean up cow pies before the games.

"That doesn't happen where I come from," I said.

The Fall Ball coaches are primarily the high school coaches, and the main guy, Scott Luke, talked to the parents for twenty minutes or so. Most of the players' parents were white, but there was a small contingent of Latino parents who all stood together.

"I speak a little Spanish," Scott said to the Latino group, "but a lot more English."

"Ees okay. Ees okay," several said, smiling.

The coaches organized some unusual drills, base stealing, pickoff moves, and hitting to right field. Coach Scott said, "Being Mammoth, we can't always get them out, but we can pick them off." He said the Fall Ball program has been in place for four years, and the boys are getting a lot better because "they know our system."

Julian is thirteen by Fall Ball rules, so he's with the Huskies, the "big boys," as they are referred to. He got a lot of attention being the new kid and from Southern California. "Julian knows what he's doing," Coach Scott said. "You don't get bad coaches in Southern California."

There was considerable talk about going to the Las Vegas tournament. Although the mothers tried to convince me that this was going to be a lot different from what we have in San Diego ("or any city really, a lot more relaxed"), I'm not so sure—it struck me more like travel ball than the kind of flimsy Fall Ball we had in Del Mar.

The kids share helmets, bats, and gloves. There are no persnickety concerns about lice or personal possessiveness. It's a small community, and you've got to share your stuff. In Mammoth the kids wear a variety of baseball pants, unlike in Del Mar where the parents are instructed in not just the color of the pants, but the color of the required belt and the piping that runs down the side of the pants. Down south, if it isn't specified by the coach, a flurry of emails from stressed baseball moms will ensue, inquiring about the details. It's a relief to put it all in better perspective.

The atmosphere was casual and friendly. The kids seem to play multiple sports—most also play soccer, and several came over after the swim meet, bearing ribbons. Practices have been scheduled so as not to conflict with soccer practices because "we want them to be able to do both." Scott mentioned that soccer has exploded in popularity in the last four years. "It's over six hundred kids now," he said. That's nearly 10 percent of the total population!

When I inquired about soccer, one of the mothers gave me the number of the northeastern something-something commissioner of soccer.

"That sounds like someone high up," I said, "I just want—"

"That's okay," she said, "In a small town, we go straight to the top. We don't mess around."

Monday

Help is on the way! Dave and Christine are coming for a visit and will bring us supplies from Trader Joe's. It's going to be better than Christmas!

We've been experimenting with various ways to get to school. I was unable to find a cut through on the north side of Meridian. The houses and A-frames are jammed onto all those lots very higgledy-piggledy, and there are no alleys or paths through there. They are definitely inhabited by people who live here, and I drew some curious looks as I was cruising through.

Tom has found a way to go through the original Snowcreek Condos, so we came back that way this morning. There's a little path through the hedge between the condo access road and the "other" Majestic Pines, on the south side of Chair 15. Then it's quick work to get home. We saw two dumpsters that had been ransacked by bears during the night. But no bears.

It's interesting how the mountains change colors at different times of day. They are fuzzy and gray in the morning, an effect I remember from the Jura Mountains when I lived in Saint-Genis-Pouilly, France, as a girl. My mother and I would often comment on the varied appearance of the mountains. Near mountains in shadow can look very black and shiny while mountains in the distance appear more blue. Mammoth Mountain developer Dave McCoy observed in his biopic, "Every day there's a difference in the place you saw yesterday. It's kind of mystic in that aspect."

The days have been sunny, but the temperatures are chilly. Mammoth is in a severe drought, and we're only supposed to water on certain days depending on your address and before 7:00 a.m. or after 10:00 p.m. The most irrigation I see is for the condo complexes and golf courses—in other words, by people who live here for the pleasure of people who visit.

Tuesday

After a week, we are getting better acclimated to the elevation and dry mountain air. The kids have had a few nosebleeds, especially Luc, but that's because he treats water as though it shouldn't actually be swallowed. Tom still gets breathless, but that doesn't seem to stop him from biking everywhere and working like a dog. And I finally slept all the way through the night. We've had an easier time than I expected, but we still struggle with dry lips and dry skin. I told Tom, "Every time I put my hand down, I want there to be a Chap Stick there." We are also mostly accustomed to the 7:40 a.m. school start time—it's already bright and sunny when we leave the house at 7:15 a.m. right now.

Even teenagers participate in the "saying hi" practice here. I noticed yesterday at the Cast Off that all the teenagers coming into the store greeted the ladies who run the cash registers. This morning, I said "hi" to a teenage boy walking to school, and he turned and said, "Good morning," and smiled. *Would this happen back home?* Maybe he guessed I live here.

I have not seen any homeless people here, but we did cross paths with a guy on a bike this morning who looked like he might have just emerged from a cave in the mountainside. He also grinned in greeting, showing that he still had a couple of teeth.

Wednesday

A neighbor near our house in Del Mar wrote that a friend who lives in Mammoth "had bears in his garage the other day." Note the plural. Tom has been working in the garage with the door open for a week while he's clearing out the attic. I wonder if I should put some caution tape around the entrance, or a note that says, "Dear bears, no food here. Just junk."

My sister emailed, "Someone told me yesterday that the strategy for avoiding brown and black bears is different, but that eye contact should be avoided for both. True?"

I wrote back, "Not sure about that. I did read that you should use different strategies for run-of-the-mill bears versus grizzlies. You can try to intimidate a regular bear by making yourself big and yelling and waving your arms. Tom says the strategy for grizzlies is to not be in the same state as they are."

After receiving my latest letter, my dad commented, "It might be a good idea to keep your eye on that Little League coach who thinks it's a good disciplinary practice to choke a dog for colliding with someone while jumping for a ball. Who knows what he will do if two outfielders collide while trying to field a fly ball?" Disturbing thought, indeed.

A friend wrote, "I am waiting for the partially buried bones, half gnawed by animals, to appear at the side of the bike path, near the edge of a lovely, but raging waterway." What kind of stories do these people think I'm writing?

We took some more trash in the bike trailer to the trash place this morning. Tom especially likes making the SUVs dropping off kids for school stop so our trash can go by. On the way home, we passed a guy running with a stroller. "He's probably got trash in there," Tom said.

I had thrown away some stale pistachio nuts, which Tom intelligently retrieved and put out for the birds; the nuts attracted a Steller's jay, who spent the next seventy-two hours gorging on them. They are all gone now, and the jay is sulking. We have a notable number of squirrels and chipmunks in the yard. It's impressive to watch them go after the pine nuts, plucking off the "leaves" of the pinecone one after another, just as fast as they can go. The tiny chipmunks mostly appear to be of uniform cuteness, but we have one who is missing most of his tail, so I can see that he does, indeed, hang around our house a lot. Tom discovered a large stash of something stored by an animal in the garage attic. He thought at first it might be some kind of exotic nut. Then he was hoping that it wasn't rat poison. After more analysis, we concluded that it was dog food. We probably just wiped out a month of hard labor by some poor survivalist, preparing for the winter.

Thursday

Yesterday, Tom and Julian came upon a bike-riding family just as the boy blew through a stop sign, provoking his father to yell after him, "Look both ways, dumbass!" Now all instructions in our family are preceded or followed by this endearment. With love, of course.

Dave and Christine showed up, bearing loads of Trader Joe's supplies and homegrown tomatoes, figs, and squash, as well as homemade jams and apple butter. Whee! Unfortunately, I can't eat it all at once because I did buy a scale. Rite Aid had two, and I bought the cheaper. Maybe I should have gotten the more expensive one because a never-before-seen number appeared under my feet when I weighed myself. Tom says I should have left on the protective sticker which read optimistically "124.5."

Dave and Christine are going backpacking in Yosemite for five or six days depending on how fast they hike. Tonight, they carefully packed their bear canister with rich, lightweight foods, including dried fruit, beef jerky, hummus, tuna, nuts, instant mashed potatoes, and small bottles of oily sauces. There is very little gluten. They cook over a four-cup Jetboil stove and share a spoon. They know the weight in ounces of every item they carry, including their tooth powder. Their packs are light except for the bear canister which weighs fifteen pounds, allowing one-and-a-half pounds per person per day. They use a water purifier and carry bleach as a backup. Dave says if the food gets lost or eaten by a bear, the trick is not to think about food as you hike out. "You're not going to *starve*," he says.

Their hike will potentially take them to 11,000 feet and drop them as low as 7,000 feet. They say they carry more clothes than most people because they're often cold. They're happy we are in a heat wave. Competition for camping passes is fierce, so they will get up early to drive to Bridgeport to get two of the twenty-five passes that are issued daily.

They told a story of a friend who hung his food bag from a tree (which apparently is against the rules now) but couldn't keep it out of the clutches of an intrepid bear. The friend went on a hunt to retrieve the stuff sack in the morning and found a food bag graveyard nearby. Apparently, in the bear's mind, he had to hide the bags or people would stop putting up new ones. They also told a story of a woman who woke up with a bear licking her mouth. Lesson: Do NOT wear cherry-flavored Chap Stick. We told the story of the bear who was photographed inside the Mammoth Lakes Vons, checking out the apple bin. It was clearly a welcoming place—after all, the automatic doors had opened wide for him.

Illustration - Bear at Vons

BEARS BEARS BEARS

"I'm not a criminal," said Paddington, hotly. "I'm a bear!"

~ Michael Bond, *A Bear Called Paddington*

Before they all denned for the winter, the bears gave us two more stories, both sad. In one mysterious situation, bear tracks were discovered leading up to the pond at the Snowcreek Condos, which was frozen over except for a big hole in the ice where the bear tracks ended. There were no tracks leading back out. And there was no bear under the ice (divers went in to look—can you imagine having that job?). Ted Carleton, writing for the *Sheet*, speculated that the bear was abducted by Martians.

In a non-alien, just-stupid-people incident, a resident emptied his shotgun at a bear and wounded it so badly that the authorities had to kill it. The resident claimed that the bear charged him, but eyewitnesses gave a different account, and some armchair detectives pointed out that the bear was shot in the buttocks, making it the first time in natural history that a bear has charged butt first. There was speculation that alcohol was involved and that either the shooter or the bear was drunk. Or both.

Allegedly, this was only the second problem bear killed in town in twenty years, a fact I find astonishing. Whistler, a similarly sized resort town, has killed twelve bears this year alone. This single metric is a testament to the care Mammoth Lakes residents and visitors take of their bears and how successful the town's campaign of coexistence has been. Nevertheless, there are naysayers, and the latest incident stirred up strong feelings, judging by readers' comments on the news article. Some residents felt that the bear situation had gotten out of control.

"These bears are being treated with kid gloves," one person commented, "while they tear apart personal property! I love the bears, but NOT when they start to destroy my or my neighbors' personal property!"

Another wrote, "I was okay with the four bears that lived here for the first thirty-five years of my life. I am not okay with the thirty bears over the last ten years now presenting danger, damaging my property, and competing for food in our little town."

Another reader commented, "I have confronted that bear on my porch and he was not afraid of people. I had been concerned of this and my safety as I did not have such a weapon to protect me from this honorary [sic] bear."

"Sean" wrote that he was happy that a resident had the "guns and guts to do what needs to be done."

Then the pro-bear people got on the horn:

"Don't shoot the bears!"

"The bears were here first!"

"If you don't like bears, go back to LA!"

Since the bear was black and the shooter was white, other pundits said the shooting was racially motivated, predicting riots and that "golf carts will burn for this."

᙮

Mammoth's bears are all American black bears, although their fur can be colored cinnamon, blond, or chocolate. There are thirty to forty bears in the town and surrounding area, and, as is typical of mountain towns, the males vastly outnumber the females. They hang out around the campgrounds and golf courses and like to sleep in the town's culverts.

The town has undertaken a coexistent philosophy, and the "Don't Feed Our Bears" signs and stickers are omnipresent. The warning goes, "A fed bear is a dead bear" because bears that become dependent on human food can turn into nuisance bears and will have to be killed. Local officials take great pride in their bears; they have undertaken an educational campaign to teach residents and visitors to keep food away from the bears by using locking dumpsters, by using bear-proof garbage containers, and by *never* leaving food in a car. An unlocked dumpster is sure to have been investigated by a bear during the night, and the cleanup in the morning can be daunting. Bears tend to defecate when they eat or are discovered, which makes the cleanup even more icky.

A black bear, or *Ursus americanus,* is the country's smallest bear. It typically weighs between one hundred to five hundred pounds, but some have been found to weigh over one thousand pounds (how would you like to run into that on the golf course?). They are omnivores—foraging for grasses, insects, and fish—although they will eat meat if they discover it, and they occasionally kill small or newborn animals. And, as we know from Winnie-the-Pooh, they also love honey.

Bears have pretty good hearing, but their sense of smell is remarkable. The local newspaper ran a story about two cars that were broken into although the owners claimed that there was no food stored inside. In the first incident, police noticed hard candies strewn on the ground next to the car; in the second, the owner acknowledged that he had brought groceries home in the car the day before, so there might have been food *fumes*.

In other bear news, a bear discovered an unlocked dumpster along Old Mammoth Road that was used to store cooking oil until it was recycled into biofuel. The bear pushed the dumpster through the parking lot and off the sidewalk (he must have had an engineering degree), tipping it over into the street and dumping out thirty to sixty gallons of the stuff. The oil ran down into parking lots and storm drains and soaked into the asphalt, creating grease rainbows. Cars drove through it and spread the oil onto nearby streets. A dog walker said it was as slippery as a skating rink. It was reported that the grease attracted every single bear within a couple square miles, and a fireman said the bears were ignoring the traffic—they were just sitting in the street, licking the pavement. The restaurant responsible for the spill finally hired a man with a portable steam cleaner, and it took him six hours to clean the area.

～

There have been incidents of black bears attacking—and even killing—humans, but they are rare. Most black bears avoid confrontations with humans although they may "bluff charge," growling and puffing. Reported attacks are usually related to a conflict over food. If you encounter a bear, hold your ground, wave your arms, and make noise. However, never challenge one that is cornered. They don't look as though they can move very fast, but they can run much faster than humans, up to twenty-five miles per hour for short distances.

Black bears are somewhat territorial, marking trees with their claws and teeth. Relocating black bears is usually unsuccessful as they are able to return to their territory from a considerable distance. Males have larger territories, from ten to forty square miles; females have smaller territories, from one to fifteen square miles, but can defend their area more effectively. Male bears will fight during mating season or to protect their territory and can inflict significant damage with their teeth and claws, sometimes even killing their opponent.

Bears are terrific climbers and can slink along ledges, sliding on their bellies, or lumber sixty feet up a tree. They can climb along a rope or up the rock face of a canyon wall. My friend Kristen scolded me for having bird seed on our deck, especially because we suspended a helpful branch across to a nearby tree, supposedly for squirrels. "You know bears can climb, right?" she said and scowled at me. She suggested that we only feed the birds during the winter months when the bears are sleeping.

They hibernate or "den" for about five months a year—starting when the deep snow sets in—although this period can be shorter if the winter is mild. Before that, they go through a period of excessive eating, up to forty thousand calories a day, to store up fat for the long snooze, during which time they lose about 30 percent of their weight. During hibernation, a bear's temperature drops, its heart rate slows, and its breathing rate decreases from a breath every three to four seconds to once every forty-five seconds. Because they do not urinate or defecate during hibernation, nitrogen from their waste products is recycled back into their bodies to build muscle, preventing atrophy.

Sows can mate with several males during the spring mating season, and cubs from the same litter may have different fathers. As is the case for over one hundred mammals, including kangaroos, bears use a reproductive strategy called delayed implantation in which the fertilized ovum may float free in the uterus for six months. This delay allows her body to determine if her health is at risk if the pregnancy proceeds. If she does not have enough fat reserves to spare for the cub, the embryo will be absorbed by her body. If she does, the embryo will implant, and eight weeks later, the cub is born. The sows typically give birth in February to two or three cubs, weighing only about one-half pound at birth. Newborns are hairless and blind, but they grow fast on their mother's rich milk. The black bear is the only mammal who can lactate without eating.

If the winter is mild, they may emerge and forage for food though usually mother and kids stay in the den until the snow melts. By then the cubs will weigh about seven pounds. Bear cubs face many predators, including mountain lions and eagles; even adult male bears sometimes eat the youngsters. They may also die in the early spring if sufficient food is not available.

The cubs are weaned at six to eight months, but they stay with their mothers for a second year in hibernation. Videos of mother bears playing with the cubs, knocking them around and smooshing them with big paws, are entertaining. The mothers devote much time and effort in teaching the cubs how to forage and about the world.

Black bears can live eighteen to twenty years, however, most live only five years because of being killed by cars or hunters or loss of habitat. Grizzlies are the adult black bears' natural predators, but the California grizzly bear, also known as *Ursus horribilis* (great name!), was hunted to extinction during the twenties, despite its appearance on the state flag and seal and its designation as the state animal.

∾

In Mammoth Lakes, before much of the education campaign got underway, bears were so good at opening Honda hatchbacks that people joked that the bears were circulating "How to Open" instructions. One bear expert maintained that trash receptacles can only be described as bear resistant, not bear proof. "Give a bear 24 hours, and he can get into anything," he said.

After watching videos of bears breaking in through car windows and sunroofs, opening steel cans and car doors, rummaging through backpacks and bags, huffing gas out of barrels, and opening a wide variety of trash cans, I am inclined to agree. In one eye-opening video, a bear was unhappy with the inconvenient positioning of a dumpster at a Colorado restaurant. To improve access, he stood on his back legs and walked backwards, like an experienced Waste Management employee, and wheeled the dumpster twenty feet out into a better location.

One poor guy claimed he was awakened at 3:30 a.m. to discover that a bear had pushed his Toyota out of his garage, rolled it down a long hill into the woods, and completely trashed it—ripped out the dashboard, side panels, seats, headrests, sunroof. And he'd taken a big crap on the driver's seat. Maybe there was some history there.

∾

Winnie-the-Pooh, Smokey Bear, and teddy bears are all based on black bears. Christopher Robin's Winnie-the-Pooh was named after Winnipeg, a black bear that lived in the London Zoo. The original E. H. Shepard illustrations of Winnie do look like a black bear cub, in some cases, a dirty black bear cub, but Disney turned him bright yellow, made him much fatter (guess those stoutness exercises didn't do much), shortened his front legs, and turned up his nose alarmingly, so that he doesn't look much like a bear anymore. An intermediate licensee later put that stupid red shirt on him—I'm a classic Pooh fan myself.

The Smokey Bear icon was crafted during WWII when the US Forest Service launched a campaign to educate citizens about wildfire prevention because there were so few firemen left at home to fight the fires. Smokey was named after a New York fireman who had suffered burns and blindness during a rescue in the twenties. A living symbol of Smokey was created in 1950 when a black bear cub was rescued from a tree during a New Mexico wildfire. He had burns on his feet, but was nursed back to health and went to live at the National Zoo in Washington, DC, until his death in 1976. He was so popular that he received up to thirteen thousand letters per week, and the postal service gave him his own zip code. When he died, his obituary ran on the front page of the *Wall Street Journal* and in the *Washington Post*, which mentioned his "many years of government service."

Toy teddy bears were created after a cartoon was published in 1902, depicting Theodore Roosevelt apparently sparing the life of a captured black bear. The tale goes that Roosevelt had been out hunting but, unlike his companions, had been unable to shoot a bear. His hunting companions clubbed and captured one for him to shoot after it was chased to exhaustion by hounds. Roosevelt declined, saying that would be unsportsmanlike, the implication being that his mercy had spared the bear. In fact, the bear was so injured that it had to be killed anyway. Despite that gruesome beginning, a toy manu-facturer requested permission to market furry stuffed bears under the moniker Teddy's bears—shortened to teddy bears—and in five years, they grew to be wildly popular with ladies and children.

IN WHICH WE VENTURE TO BISHOP

New York, London, Paris, Bishop

~ BISHOP BUMPER STICKER

August 29–September 3, 2014

Friday

LABOR DAY WEEKEND is here, and the town is heating up in temperature and excitement: offerings include a reggae festival, a library book sale, and—judging by all the tents and signs already in place this morning on our way home from school—many outdoor end-of-season BLOWOUT store sales. At this point, however, it feels as though summer is still in full swing. We are braced for a hot weekend.

Julian was told at school that the snowboard teams will not get organized until November. The baseball people were guessing that the mountain would open around Veterans Day, the second week in November. Snow sounds fairly theoretical right now.

Saturday

I was excited to go down to Bishop for the Tri-County Fair and rodeo. The three counties are Inyo, Alpine, and Mono (pronounced mow-no, not mah-no—Dave was right; to paraphrase Spalding Gray, count on an outsider to teach you about your own locale). Driving down there was like descending into the depths of hell: 80 degrees at Toms Place, 84 at Sherwin Summit, and 92 at the bottom of Sherwin Grade.

We went to Kmart first. Even though we've been out of civilization for only two weeks, it was still a shock to walk in to lights! air conditioning! plastic stuff! We bought long pants for Julian (despite his claim that he would be all right wearing soccer shorts all winter), hangers, and trash cans for recycling—purchases short on natural materials and long on synthetics.

After Pizza 395, where the milk shakes were good and the pizza was covered with enough veggies for four pies, we ventured to the fairgrounds where the wise stayed out of the sun and as close to the free water offered by the Salvation Army as possible. The kids hated everything: the crafts barn, the animals in the petting zoo, the bluegrass band, the butterfly house where you fed butterflies with sugar water, the father-son family circus with two doves and one large cat, the rodeo—you name it, they hated it. They had no interest in riding any of the rides or playing any of the games. It's hard to know if they really hated everything or if everything pales in contrast to the lure of video games. It reminded me of the scene from *Trainspotting* in which the drug addicts attempt to go for a walk, but two minutes into the walk, it seems so dismal and flat and quiet, they head straight home to do more drugs. Much later, after the heat and drive had faded from memory, my older son, Luc, would report that the butterflies and the circus weren't so bad.

The exhibits were generally mediocre with the exception of the remarkable handmade quilts and some whimsical food arrangements that were charming. The livestock portion of the fair had taken place earlier in the month (in a ranching community, it merits its own show), so there were not many animals to see. The people watching, on the other hand, was impressive: bad dye jobs, peculiar facial hair, obscene T-shirts, and lots of cowboy hats. The carnies always look pretty rough, but here the fair attendees gave them some competition—although, it must be said, the fair in Del Mar is no beauty pageant either.

There were a number of booths selling junk mostly dominated by fake guns, cameo gear, and T-shirts of the "I eat vegetarians" and "Deer—the Real Meat" variety. The most interesting booth was one set up by Inyo County dedicated to agriculture. Its motif of "From Inyo County to Your Table" promoted a "Beef—it's what's for dinner" message and the production of vegetables, fruits, nuts, dates, and honey in the county, although it acknowledged that tourism represents a larger industry. The booth did not mention that, like all of Owens Valley, any agriculture is dependent on irrigation which means a constant tussle for water with the city of Los Angeles, part of the long fascinating history of water in Owens Valley.

The booth was staffed by a lovely outspoken albino woman named Kristina Blüm who, I found out later, is Miss City of Bishop and works at the Chamber. I noticed her partly because of her white hair and light eyes and partly because of her enthusiasm in talking about the booth displays. She was quoted in the newspaper as saying, "I can't get away with anything; I stand out," adding that standing out has its advantages. True enough, I spotted her again a few weeks later, doing some shopping at the Cast Off.

There was also a booth for Alpine County that contained a folding chair and an unopened cardboard box sitting on the floor. Tom said that apparently none of the three people who live in the county could make it down to Bishop that day.

The rodeo took place in the main arena and a small side ring. Events in the main arena included barrel racing, calf roping, bareback riding (on both bulls and horses), and an unusual timed event. In this event, someone on horseback—usually a father—came thundering down to where the "runners" stood, whipped around to lay down a piece of canvas that was already tied to his horse, and the runner—usually his daughter—flung herself on the canvas and held on for dear life as the horse raced back up the arena, dragging the canvas and girl thumping up and down on the ground.

There was an unexpected disregard for safety, even in the small arena, where little kids attempted to ride on sheep but inevitably fell off to get bumped or stepped on. Each deposed child was immediately snatched up, reset on his or her feet, and pushed off with a swat on the butt. There was another event in which all the kids' shoes and boots were thrown in a pile, and the kids had to run through the muck in their stocking feet to retrieve their shoes and then try to be first back to the start line to win a pair of cowboy boots. They raise tough kids in Bishop. In case we hadn't noticed before, we're not in Del Mar anymore.

The winner of the bareback contest (the horse variety) was a local high school boy who has won a number of state awards. He rode very well and (almost) made it look easy. His lone competitor was thrown, perhaps stomped on, and then limped away. Neither of the bull riders qualified, which means they paid an entrance fee, competed at tremendous physical risk (those bulls are *insane*), and came away with nothing. You can't be a rodeo rider for long without racking up significant medical bills and enduring chronic pain from related injuries. Watching the bareback events, a rational person thinks, *Why why why?*

The skills on display at a rodeo strike me as of dubious practical use on a ranch, though probably more useful than those from the ATV rodeo that was held on Friday night. In that event, competitors used Wiffle ball bats to whack and pop balloons attached to the other teams' vehicles in order to defeat them. In comparison, the tasks in the bobcat rodeo we went to in Iowa a few years ago seemed very applicable, except maybe putting a basketball through a hoop.

Because it was kids' day (Julian got in free!), smoking was prohibited—although enforcement appeared to end at sunset. As we were leaving, the crowd streaming into the midway was raucous and sounded ready for some heavy partying—cigarettes might be a mild indulgence compared to what they had in mind. Bishop is a different culture from Mammoth, and I imagine there is real competition between the toughened ranch kids and the mountain snowboarders with 'tude. I hope the parents don't fight at the Little League games. The Bishop parents will win.

We were able to get the Mighty 1090 on the radio on the way home, and we listened in the dark to the Padres. Alexi Amarista got the walk off RBI in the bottom of the tenth to win the series against the Dodgers and set up the potential sweep tomorrow. Go, Little Ninja!

Sunday
We rode bikes down to Shady Rest to play some baseball, Tom carrying a bucket of balls and all the sports equipment while Julian carried nothing, for reasons of awesomeness, according to him. At least *I* carried a house key and a baseball cap. Julian is starting to look like an outfielder with his confident catches and nice throws back to the infield. Now if his mother would just buy him some baseball pants that fit...

My writing room is nearly ready! Tom has built a desk in the loft, the sunniest room in the house, where I can write looking out at the pines, surrounded by games and toys. The desk is lovely, made out of a large oak plank, a gift from my mother. Tom attached it to the wall with a piano hinge and set it on two narrow tapered legs of light pecan. A big round table, a futon for napping, and my piano are all close at hand. My space is set off from the rest of the household by a flight of stairs. Stephen King says that you can write anywhere, but you have to have a door that shuts. I haven't found that to be true—I wrote most of my first book at my son's skate park and the first draft of the second book in a large coworking space with a noisy fan. Then again, I don't write like Stephen King.

Monday

The town has been very busy the last three days, and the bicycle traffic past our house quite frequent. By noon, however, the report was that US 395 carried a constant stream of cars returning to Southern California. Goodbye, those of you with full-time jobs.

We hiked up to Crystal Lake from Lake George, an ascent of about 2,000 feet, which was most welcome because of the heat at lower elevations. The hike was very pleasant, following multiple switchbacks, mostly in the shade, with lots of views of Lake George and Lake Mary (and beyond). Lake Mary was crowded with boats, primarily motor boats, while Lake George, restricted to nonmotorized vessels, held only a few kayaks and paddleboats and boards. Crystal Lake is gorgeous, clear and deep blue, snuggled down under Crystal Crag and surrounded by dramatic treeless rocky ridges.

On the way back, Julian encouraged us to hurry by calling out, "Let's go, cupcakes!" in imitation of his Gym teacher who allegedly bikes alongside the boys on their one-and-a-half-mile run along the forest trail behind their school. "Pick it up, Crittenden!" Julian bellowed. He said the Gym teacher calls them all by their last names—a slight change in approach from Mr. Philip in Del Mar.

On the trail, we made the acquaintance of a family from Paradise, a tiny community between Mammoth and Bishop. When they heard that Julian is at the middle school, the dad asked, "Do you know the twins?" Of course Julian did—small town.

The dad is from Mexico City. He is burly, talkative, and lively. His wife is lithe and more reserved. She is originally from the Bay Area, but they have lived here nineteen years. She teaches at a Christian school in Bishop. She said delicately that the public schools in Bishop don't have a good reputation. They lived briefly in Mammoth, but "we didn't make it," she said. *That* piqued my interest.

"What do you mean, you didn't make it?" I asked.

"Oh, I shouldn't have said that," she said. Upon further questioning, it appears that the pressure of snow and a daily commute to Bishop made them decide to move further downhill. They also lived in Cape Cod for one year but came back after ten months.

"What did you miss?" I asked.

"The mountains," she said.

"The *outdoors*," her husband said, "the air, everything."

Their kids seemed happy in the mountains too and showed us the pumice they had found and told us to put our feet in at the lake when we got there. As we talked about the community and mountain biking, the mother said that when they visited Mexico, the contrast between the rich and the poor was very apparent. When they returned home, she said she was struck by the sight of these great big empty houses, owned by people who don't live here, while some Latinos were digging in a ditch by the side of the road.

"I thought, *it's the same thing here.* You don't expect to see that in America," she said.

Tuesday

Another beautiful ride to school, startling the Steller's jays and scattering the tiny chipmunks across the bike paths. One unbeautiful part was encountering a mound of bear scat on the hill up to the library. Scat doesn't seem like the right description for a big, wet pile of brown and yellow ickiness. It did appear to contain a lot of nuts and husks, rather than ham and granola bars.

I went for a walk this afternoon, up to the Twin Lakes campground (near where we saw the bear last year lying on the beach, with his head in a cooler, lethargically gnawing on someone's lunch) and back down Old Mammoth Road. It was a very long walk and had turned into a trudge by the end. I saw an adorable fuzzy baby deer who appeared to be on his own. I was surprised that there would be such a young deer at this time of year. And I saw a female deer a little later who stared at me for as long as I was willing to stand still and be stared at.

Tom and Julian brought me an unopened can of beer that they found on the way home from school, although Julian first claimed that it had been distributed as part of school lunch. I have been reading the police reports to see what dangers lurk in our community, and it appears that alcohol is often involved: one drunk guy got into a knife fight with his brother; another was arrested for urinating in public, although he allegedly was so drunk he could hardly stand up; a woman was found passed out along Meridian Boulevard (not the best place to be passed out); and some intoxicated guys got in trouble for harassing female patrons at a local eatery. A Jeep was driven off the road into the bushes by a drunk driver in a car accident on US 395. The driver's wife then attempted to drive the car back onto the road, but she also was too drunk to drive. Both were charged with DUI.

On the positive side, there was little else in the police reports: a few minor incidents involving a stolen credit card, a missing cell phone, a Peeping Tom (who might have been drunk), and a kicked-in door. I wonder if crime here is very low, even burglary, because the people who live here don't want to get caught doing something and lose their jobs. Also there are almost no homeless, and the transients are too wealthy to steal—well, they may still steal, but they're not interested in stealing TVs, guns, and bicycles.

Wednesday

When we picked up Taff at Snowcreek for baseball practice, Julian spotted five deer. I thought at first that he had said, "Oh dear!" until I realized it was "Oh, deer!" He said one had enormous antlers.

I have now ridden with Taff twice all the way down to Whitmore and back, and here's what I have to say: if you have a secret, do not tell it to Taff. He talks nonstop. Within ten minutes of meeting him, I learned his height, weight, and how much weight he had lost because of the medication he is on.

"Like I'm not even hungry," he said. "Like, you could put a piece of pizza in front of me, and I wouldn't even feel hungry. Or I would take one bite, and then I would get a stomachache and wouldn't want to eat anymore." He reported that the medication also keeps him up at night. "It'll be like 3:30 in the morning, and I can't sleep," he said.

I couldn't resist asking why he was taking this terrible medication.

"ADD," he said. "I'm really scattered, aren't I, Julian? You've seen me, right? Like I moved my cup like five times during lunch today. One time I even *lost* it. And I talk a lot, right? I like talking. I think it's boring when no one is talking."

Julian read and listened with only half an ear but came to when he detected a significant pause, indicating that Taff had asked a question that required an answer. On the way home last week, Taff fell silent for a period of approximately thirty seconds, and Julian stirred. "Taff?" he said. "Are you all right? I think that's the longest I've ever heard you go without talking."

Today Taff joyfully recounts this incident. "'That's the longest I've ever heard you go...' Do you think that's true, Julian? Do you think that's the longest I've gone without talking? Except when I'm in school, right?"

He is full of energy—and slightly indiscreet information, including tidbits about his father's guns, his hunting history, and their plans to scare off the local coyotes. "I'm not really a gun-type person," Taff says. "I don't really like being around them. Like, especially when my sisters are around, I don't really want to hold them. Or do anything with them, really." He turns quickly to other topics.

"I'll be so glad when the tourists are gone," he says. He pronounces it "tour-ists."

"They pretty much are gone," says Julian, looking up from his book.

"Not really," says Taff. "Haven't you noticed how *slow* the Internet is?"

He has remarkable explanations for everything. "*Ender's Game* was based on *Star Wars*, only it wasn't as good—that's why I didn't read it."

Julian engages: "*Ender's Game* wasn't based on *Star Wars*! They're totally different."

"Nuh-uh," Taff says hotly. "They're both about *the chosen one* [he says this with derision] and how he has to fight some evil guy and then he wins. I think stuff like that is boring."

They argued about this for a while, but the issue was left unresolved. I did, however, learn precisely which *Star Wars* movies Taff thinks are good and why.

Fall Ball practice continues to be a fairly casual affair. Some parents were encouraging a mother to throw a wallpaper removal party in the house she has just moved into.

"Get some beer and wine, and we'll knock that out in a weekend," one said.

"Git 'er done," said another.

In a reminder of where we come from, an out-of-towner blasted in today like a strong gust from Southern California with her new car, blonde hair, very white teeth, and other fine attributes. She bounced over to introduce herself—friendly, but an alien from a distant land.

Dave and Christine made it back! They showed up in early evening and headed straight for the showers. We watched them unpack the bear canister that contained a few small corners of food in baggies. They pronounced this "plenty" for one more day. Nevertheless, they were happy to see salad and fresh fruit—"any kind of food, really," they said. They did not see a bear, suffered no injuries, and their biggest problem was the crowd at the Riviera, one of the lakesides where there were eleven people. Tom suggested that they keep their remaining food in the bear canister—just in case one breaks into our kitchen. It's no surprise that they survived, but I was relieved, having spent some time learning about others who had run afoul of our mountains.

Illustration - The Minarets

ABSENS ET INDAGANS

But we little know until tried how much of the uncontrollable there is in us, urging across glaciers the torrents, and up dangerous heights, let the judgment forbid as it may.

~ JOHN MUIR, *THE MOUNTAINS OF CALIFORNIA*

By EARLY AUGUST 2013, his posters were everywhere in Mammoth Lakes: on the shuttles, in the store windows, at the grocery and the post office, at trailheads, in the Welcome Center, and at the police station and the library. "MISSING since July 17, 2013, MATTHEW GREENE," they said. Pictured was a pleasant-looking blue-eyed man with thinning sandy hair. The details were sparse: Matt had been staying at Shady Rest Campground and had vanished, leaving his camping gear behind. Some friends had been with him, but they left town after his Subaru developed mechanical problems. Matt was hanging around for a few more days while his car was being repaired; then he planned to meet up with friends in Colorado.

A serious hiker and climber, he was likely to have headed into the mountains, but his family and friends had no idea which direction he might have gone. With so little to go on, the authorities conducted a general search, but turned up nothing. The newspapers ran articles reporting on the lack of progress and cautioned their readers to "always let your friends know where you're going when you venture into the wilderness."

I'm sure I wasn't the only stranger who stared at Matt's photo on the shuttle and wondered, *Matt, where are you? What happened?*

⁓

Eighty years earlier, on August 7, 1933, the father of another out-doorsman waited anxiously for his son at Glacier Lodge, an outpost on the eastern side of the Sierra, between Owens Valley and the crest. The father, Walter Starr Sr., was himself an accomplished mountain-eer; in 1886, he and a companion were the first to trek through the High Sierra from Yosemite down to Kings Canyon on pack animals. By 1933, as a wealthy, prominent attorney in the Bay Area, he had strong ties to the Sierra Club, Ansel Adams, and Francis Farquhar who would play an important role in the conservation movement during the forthcoming decade. Starr's two sons had inherited his love of the Sierra, and both were frequent visitors to the Range of Light. His older son, Walter Starr Jr., known by his nickname Peter, was especially devoted to the wilderness and used his weekends and vacations for camping and climbing. On this occasion, the plan had been for Peter to spend ten days in the mountains, exploring the trails and peaks along the John Muir Trail, and resupply at Glacier Lodge on August 7, where he would meet his father and then continue on his own, wandering for another week.

He didn't show up on August 7. He didn't show up on August 8. On August 9, Walter decided to head back to the city. He was dis-turbed that Peter didn't appear, but thought it very possible that

Peter had decided to investigate some new trails or had found something of great interest. After all, he wasn't due back at work until August 14, a week later. Perhaps he had decided to take advantage of the extra time; in those days, it would have been very difficult to notify his father of the change of plans. In our age of "text me when you get there"—what I call "progress-through-life" constant communication—it's hard to understand such a casual attitude, but that's how it was back then. You just didn't know where everyone was all the time. Besides, Walter considered, his son was an extraordinarily experienced mountaineer. If anyone would walk out of the woods just a few days late and unscathed, it would be Peter.

Peter had begun accompanying his father on his outdoor adventures at a young age. By the time he was in college, he was spending most of his free time in the mountains. By age thirty, he had summited forty peaks or more and documented his experiences, detailing the difficulty, distances, and elevation changes of various trails and routes—his passion is palpable in his copious notes. A track star in college, Peter had maintained his fitness and could hike and climb at a pace that would exhaust most recreational enthusiasts. On two occasions, arriving at a summit and discovering that the usual pencil was missing from the register can, he used blood from his ear to scrawl his entry. He was no wimp. A photo from that time shows a tall, startlingly good-looking man, grinning confidently at the camera, dressed in a sleeveless white T-shirt, khaki knickers, knee-high socks, and basketball shoes—the climber's attire of the period. Although he had an outgoing nature and enjoyed a close circle of fraternity brothers and friends, he liked to be in the mountains by himself. He usually climbed alone and never used a rope.

After completing both his undergraduate and law degrees at

Stanford, he traveled in Europe and Africa for nine months. Among his adventures, romantic and otherwise, he had summited Mont Blanc, the treacherousness of which he described in a letter to his father. It read in part,

> Upon arriving at the refuge, I had one of the shocks of my life. I had always imagined the summit of Mont Blanc to be a nicely rounded dome, in fact it appears as such from Chamonix. But it was evident that what appeared to be flat from below was a steep sawtooth ridge with hardly room to stand on it. Due to the sharpness of the arete, the top was absolutely not the least bit flat but came to a pointed ridge along which one walked pigeon toed with one foot on one side, the other on the other. Thousands of feet dropped on either side as approximate to perpendicularity as possible below to glaciers below on either side—solid ice so no feeling of security. If anyone slid, I don't see how the others could hold on as the ice picks made practically no entry into the surface.

Peter had gone to work at a large San Francisco firm after passing the bar, but he continued to spend as much time as possible in the mountains. The Eastern Sierra was the subject of his intense interest. His current project was an ambitious one-person effort to identify and document the whole region south of Yosemite along the John Muir Trail, including the Minaret Range. His goal was to publish a detailed guide for hikers and climbers of the vast array of trails and routes through the area. As of 1933, four years into the project, he had accomplished the bulk of that work and was pushing to finish.

During an afternoon in late July, he entertained a fraternity brother on the day before his wedding, swimming and playing tennis. Peter himself had never married. The following afternoon, after attending the wedding, he left, as his mother wrote in her diary, "on his vacation to his beloved mountains."

∽

Matthew Greene himself was no outdoor novice. He grew up in rural Pennsylvania where access to meadows, woods, and streams was abundant. His father was the dam tender at a lake near the family's home, so his kids were allowed into areas normally not open to the public. He was an outdoors enthusiast, and Matt accompanied him on numerous fishing trips. Despite being eight years her senior, Matt was attentive to his younger sister and took her fishing and hiking although she has said "he was hell to keep up with." By adulthood, he had developed a taste for climbing, hiking, and biking.

After graduating from Penn State, he taught school in Colorado at a facility for disadvantaged youths and began spending as much time as possible in the wilderness. In 1998, he joined the Peace Corps and lived for three years in Papua New Guinea. His letters home regaled his friends and family with stories of rustic living, adventures in the outback, stumbling across a pit full of human remains, and dozens of extraordinary photographs of exotic landscapes and breathtaking views.

In one from Australia, he reported on his "journey to become a jungle savage." He wrote,

> [Sugar]cane grows monstrous in these parts. When I walk
> from place to place it's not uncommon for a native to cut
> me a stalk eight feet tall with the girth of the fat part of a

javelin. You don't actually eat it, but rather chew on the sweet center part and then spit it out. Moral of the story—I've learned how to make short work of an enormous stalk of cane, and there's nothing better to re-energize you on a long hike. When I went skydiving, our landing zone was in a tiny strip of grass among the vast fields of cane, which happens to be Queensland's major crop. They produce so much of the stuff that the farms have mini-railroads to cart it around. But it's a different variety than the [Papua New Guinea] type— not much taller than 5 feet and as skinny as your thumb. After we landed and the parachutes had been repacked, one instructor hopped up on a passing cane train and grabbed a few stalks for everyone, only about a foot long. I forgot all about pesticide, ripped the sides off in a full swoop with my teeth, chewed the sweetness out of the center, and tossed the rubbish on a garbage heap—all in a matter of 10-15 seconds. As I wiped my mouth I looked up to find everyone was staring at me like I just drank out of the toilet bowl or something. They must've thought I'd been raised by wolves.

After his Peace Corps stint, Matt taught high school math in Nazareth, Pennsylvania, about seventy-five miles north of Philadelphia. He had been there twelve years and was a popular teacher, well liked by his students and colleagues. He loved spending his free time in nature, as did several of his fellow teachers, and they frequently hiked and climbed together. Although he had a close-knit group of friends, at thirty-nine years of age, Matt was a bachelor, independent, and accustomed to being alone.

A fit athlete, he ran the Boston Marathon in 2007, finishing with a very respectable time of 3:07, and placing 1,602 out of 20,348, despite rain, cold temperatures, and high winds. He had a reputation as a speedy hiker and a careful, critical thinker in the wild. In a letter home, he described his ascent up Australia's Mount Sorrow, set in the Daintree National Park rainforest, as "a jumble of 2000+ foot jungle-covered mountains alive with tales of trekkers setting off on hikes never to be heard from again." Although the round trip was esti-mated to require seven hours, Matt completed it in three. He scoffed, "It wouldn't have taken me seven hours if I was wearing shackles."

As was his habit, as soon as school let out, he had driven out to California to meet up with his friends from Pennsylvania, Jill and John, arriving in Mammoth Lakes on June 27. The three of them threw themselves into rock climbing nearly every day, biting off Crystal Crag, Clark Canyon, Iris Slab, Gong Show Crag, and Benton Crags. They completed two significant ice climbs: North Peak and the V-Notch Couloir on Polemonium, a hair-raising 1,200-foot rope ascent that required traversing the glacier.

Matt had started having car trouble on the drive out to Cali-fornia and discovered when he took the car into the repair shop in Mammoth Lakes that his Subaru had blown a head gasket. Jill and John first intended to wait for the repair, but the shop kept pushing out the date it would be completed. Matt urged them to go on and said that he would be in touch. He was used to doing his own thing and wasn't concerned about staying behind. They departed reluc-tantly on July 7. The next day Matt started soloing in the Minarets. He climbed Reigeluth and Clyde on July 8 and July 11, respectively. His last annotated climb was Unicorn Peak on July 13.

Records would show later that he made a credit card purchase on July 17 at the Rite Aid drugstore. He went to the library and used their computers to post on a climbing website. He talked to his parents and placed a call to the car repair place at 4:33 p.m. He sent a light-hearted text to his friends about 8:30 p.m., saying all was well. His cell phone recorded a text message from a pal back in Pennsylvania at 3:00 a.m. although it was unclear if that was the time of receipt or the time of transmission. It's a question we will never know the answer to. Matt was never heard from again.

~

When Peter Starr didn't show up for work on August 14, 1933, a week after he missed his appointment with his father, his family and colleagues snapped into action. They alerted the police, and Peter's senior partner at the law firm arranged an immediate lunch meeting with Francis Farquhar, president of the Sierra Club and a well-known business man who had a wide network of contacts in Northern California. Farquhar recognized that time was of the essence and promptly notified the nearby ranger stations and began to spread the word that help was urgently needed to locate Peter.

The first challenge the searchers faced was that they didn't know where Peter was going. It was only known that he had planned to travel over Tioga Pass to the east side of the Sierra for a multi-day exploration ending with a rendezvous with his father ten days later at Glacier Lodge. Authorities began searching for his car at all the trailheads and dead-end roads from Yosemite down to Mammoth Lakes. Late on August 14 they found it at Agnew Meadows, the trailhead that serves as the gateway to Ritter Range and the Minarets. This jagged saw blade of craggy peaks forms the most dramatic skyline of the Eastern Sierra—dark, brutal, and very dangerous.

Farquhar concluded from the timeline that if Peter was still alive, he would have survived by staying near water, and the best way to quickly find him would be to search by air. Peter's law firm arranged to borrow a biplane from one of the firm's clients, and Farquhar took off with a pilot to scour the rugged terrain near lakes and waterways for any signs of Peter. It is clear from the aerial photographs Farquhar took of their reconnaissance that it was like looking for a needle in a haystack—the number of crags, chutes, and crannies is overwhelming, and the scale of the mountains such that a man, or his body, could be hidden for weeks without being found.

At the same time, Farquhar had engaged the services of two gifted young climbers, Jules Eichorn and Glen Dawson. Eichorn had been introduced to mountain climbing by his piano teacher, who happened to be Ansel Adams. In 1927, at a Sierra Club mountaineering camp, Eichorn met Dawson who, like himself, was fifteen years old. Over the next few years, they formed a sterling climbing partnership, beginning what some describe as the golden era of Sierra mountaineering. During the summer of 1930, they climbed no fewer than eighteen peaks in the region. Returning the next year, they thrilled the mountaineering world by summiting three Minarets in one day: Clyde, Michael, and a third, which was subsequently named Eichorn Minaret. Similar exploits followed in 1932. In 1933, at the age of twenty-one, they climbed three separate peaks of the Devils Crags when a tremendous storm forced them to bivouac (sleep with a minimum of equipment) on a ledge before their triumphant descent into camp. They had just returned from this trip when they received an alert from Farquhar. In the afternoon of August 14, he sent a wire to Dawson in Los Angeles, asking him to ready himself for a trip north, and telephoned Eichorn in San Francisco with the same message. A day later they would begin their journey up to the Eastern Sierra to look for Peter Starr.

Farquhar also notified a Sierra packer that he would need the services of Norman Clyde, a Sierra mountain man reputed for many things, including his search and rescue abilities. Since he was exploring the nearby Palisades Glacier, the packer left a letter for him at Glacier Lodge, ending, "The man's [sic] that is lost is [Peter] Starr. Father will pay all wages and expenses. They need you very much. Be sure to go."

By nightfall on August 15, Eichorn, Dawson, and Clyde were joined by over a dozen authorities, volunteers, friends, and family members. Twenty strong, it was possibly the finest search and rescue team assembled in Sierra history. They converged on Ediza Lake because Peter's campsite had been discovered just below. It is a beautiful scenic spot, just a three-hour hike from Agnew Meadows. Peter's name was on items in the camp, and some belongings were identified as his. There was, however, no sign of Peter. Further investigation uncovered that as early as a week before, some miners in the area had noticed that the camp had been abandoned. They allegedly had notified somebody, but no one had attempted to discover what had happened to the missing camper.

Meanwhile, the news about Peter had been picked up by the press. The story that a handsome, bachelor attorney from a wealthy family had disappeared during a solo-expedition was compelling, and articles reporting on the search ran in newspapers in San Francisco, Los Angeles, the Central Valley, and Owens Valley over the next days.

∾

Jill and John attempted to reach Matt periodically on his cell phone after July 17. They sent texts and left messages when he didn't pick up, assuming that his phone had run out of battery power, or that he was in areas without signal, a common occurrence in the high mountains around Mammoth Lakes. When he didn't meet up with his friends in Colorado as planned, they became concerned. Meanwhile Matt's mother was trying to reach him, but all her calls were going directly to voice mail. Calls started going out to other friends and Matt's parents, and it became clear that no one had heard from Matt for over ten days. Matt's brother-in-law later reported to the press that they felt, "This is strange. This is unlike Matt. He is a highly meticulous person." Something was really wrong.

It turned out his car had been waiting to be picked up at the shop for over a week. His camping equipment was still at the campground although Matt had paid for the site only through July 17. Campground staff had packed up his belongings and stored them. They had alerted the police to the situation, but no one had attempted to find the missing camper.

Now alarmed, Jill and John contacted the Mammoth Lakes Police Department, and Detective Hornbeck notified his family. Matt was formally reported missing on July 29. On August 1, the detective informed the family that the Mono County Sheriff's Search and Rescue (SAR) Team didn't have enough information to start a search.

"The area where we're talking about is so vast it isn't even funny," an undersheriff of the Mono County Sheriff's Office was quoted in the press.

"So far, nothing has come back giving us a location to even start." Hornbeck told ABCNews.com, "We're just hoping that some climbers or hikers will come across him somewhere." He had placed flyers with Matt's photo at some strategic locations. It was also reported that the police believed Matt might have gotten a ride with someone to a climbing site.

A group of Matt's friends headed straight out to Mammoth Lakes to get involved. Because of the challenge of the terrain, the dangers of the stark peaks, melting glaciers, and rockslides, searchers would be limited to experienced climbers. Matt's family cautioned well-intentioned volunteers to please be careful—they didn't want anyone else to get hurt. Matt's family set up a donation site for funds to support independent search and rescue efforts and travel costs for volunteers—and to defray costs for the "worst-case scenario."

It was known among Matt's friends that when he departed on a day hike, he would frequently pull out the relevant pages from R. J. Secor's climbing guide and take them with him. Upon his return, he would reinsert them into his book. Back in town and searching through the book, his pals discovered that several pages were missing related to the series of peaks from Banner and Ritter through the two-mile-long expanse of peaks and canyons of the Minaret range. It narrowed down the search somewhat, but not much.

Mono County issued a press release stating that because the search area surrounding Banner and Ritter was outside the county, SAR had not been officially activated. The sheriff's department sent a ground crew to look around the bases of Banner and Ritter, and the California Highway Patrol (CHP) used a training exercise to search in the area with a helicopter, including the Minarets. Neither effort turned up any clues. The county notified Madera County and Yosemite Park officials that a climber might be in their area. Staff also began emailing people who had signed up for recent Forest Service camping permits to see if anyone might have seen Matt.

Matt's family launched a Facebook page and a social media campaign to raise awareness about his disappearance. Through their efforts, newspapers began to run articles about him, and the *Los Angeles Times*, the *San Diego Union-Tribune*, *ABC News*, and news outlets in Pennsylvania provided coverage. The reporters interviewed authorities and family members.

Matt's sister, Tiffany, was quoted as saying, "We can't visualize him getting himself into any kind of dangerous situation. He's the personality type who would just turn back if it was too dangerous."

When a Lehigh Valley news outlet asked Matt's mother if he could survive two weeks in the wild, she paused. "It's possible. It's just that it's so long. No matter how good you are, no one is invincible," she said.

∽

In the modern era, the investigation into a case like Matt's would fall to emergency responders, such as local Search and Rescue. All counties in the US are required by law to provide emergency services to residents and visitors. Mono County Sheriff's SAR Team was established in 1966 and was originally called the June Lake Mountain Rescue Team. The group is comprised of unpaid volunteers from the community and is managed by a sheriff's deputy. The team typically undertakes about fifty missions per year, ranging from lost hikers and fallen rock climbers to missing skiers and injured snowmobilers. They train in search, tracking, rock rescue, navigation, CPR, and first aid. Specialists also receive training for swift water, avalanches, ice climbing, search dogs, helicopter and snowmobile rescues, and diving in open water and under ice. Their motto is: "Where roads end, we begin…"

The group maintains an elaborate website, reporting on operations, personnel, donations, and training. According to the website, their process requires verification of a point where the missing person was last seen. The rescuers then track in a widening circle from that point. Their philosophy is that they look for clues, not people. Then the clues will lead to the person. That may be their stated method, but after reading dozens of mission reports, it seemed to me that more frequently they find out where the person was coming from or heading to, or a phone call or text message is received stating the person's location, and they go there. Matt's case presented a challenge for two reasons—both surprising, in this day and age: his car and his phone were both disabled, giving no clue as to his point of departure, his location, or his destination.

Detective Hornbeck told the Lehigh Valley newspaper that other factors contributed to the difficulty of searching for Matt. He said that there had been three days of bad weather in mid-July, causing flash floods in the backcountry mountain canyons. The bodies of people caught in flash floods may not be found for weeks, even years, he stated. He further pointed to a fire burning twenty-five miles away whose smoke was blocking the view of the mountains and would interfere with the search dogs' ability to follow a scent. And he said the terrain was too treacherous for dogs. "The word is out," Hornbeck said, "but we haven't heard anything yet." On August 6, he told the *Mammoth Times*, "My hands are tied. We don't have any more leads."

Hornbeck also told the press that incidents of missing hikers were common. What was uncommon in this situation was the experience and cautious nature of the missing hiker. Indeed, on August 20, 2013, a forty-seven-year-old Bishop man was reported missing when he failed to return home by 8:00 p.m. He had called his family around noon from Round Valley Peak, saying that he would be home in a few hours. SAR personnel found his body late on August 21. He had fallen down a 30-foot rock chute above Tamarack Lakes, approximately three miles from the site of his last phone call. He and his wife had purchased a home in Swall Meadows a few months before and moved from New York City to live his dream of a climbing life in the Eastern Sierra. He was a former Inyo County SAR member. Assisting in the search were Inyo County SAR, CHP helicopter H-80 out of Apple Valley, Mono County SAR, and China Lake Mountain Rescue Group.

Meanwhile, the news about Matt spread to some mountaineering websites, and serious outdoors people began to get involved. They checked the summit records at Lyell, Banner, and Ritter and reported that Matt had not registered. Information began to flow in concerning areas that had been searched without success. Then it was discovered that, although Matt had departed with a daypack leaving behind his tent, stove, heavy coat, and bivouac, he had taken a mountaineering axe and crampons with him. This news reached Dean Rosnau, a search and rescue expert, who was familiar with the glaciers in the Minarets.

⌒⌒

Peter and Matt were not alone in being drawn to the Minarets; the dramatic beauty and mystery of the range have long beckoned to those who yearn to test themselves in the wilderness. One of the most recognizable sections of the Sierra Nevada is the fraternity formed by Mount Ritter and Banner Peak. At 13,157 feet high, Mount Ritter is the highest of the two and distinguished by its symmetrical pyramid shape. A saddle containing snow most of the year joins it to Banner Peak, whose top is more dome-like and only slightly lower at 12,945 feet. Mount Ritter was named for a German geographer by the California Geological Survey, who was responsible for naming many of the peaks in the area. John Muir was the first to summit Mount Ritter, a feat he accomplished in 1872, and his account of being paralyzed by fear and unable to move either up or down while spread-eagled on one of its sheer faces is riveting. Banner Peak was named for the clouds that seem to fly from its peak.

Continuing to the south, one's eye discovers an even more striking result of ancient volcanic eruption and glacial carving. The narrow spires of the Minarets rise starkly from their chutes, thrusting aggressively into the sky like inverted black icicles. If they were part of the landscape of a fantasy novel, they would surely be the lair of a mythical dragon or a powerful warlock.

The Minarets were first known only by number, but gradually, as persistent and wily mountaineers found ways to reach their tops without falling prey to their landslides, glaciers, and sheer faces absent of handholds or footholds, they were named after those who arrived first. Clyde Minaret, the highest Minaret, was named after the esteemed climber Norman Clyde who was called to help search for Peter Starr. Clyde first climbed its 12,281 feet in 1928.

Michael Minaret was named after a Yosemite postmaster and his schoolteacher wife who climbed the 12,276 foot peak together in 1923 while camping at Ediza Lake. Exploring westward, they discovered a notch in the crest through which they could pass to the other side of the Minarets. They then found a chute which they managed to follow up to Michael's dizzying heights. As they approached the summit, the husband became concerned about his wife's safety and begged her to wait while he completed the last section, which he described as "the most difficult 300 feet that I ever had the pleasure of climbing." The couple had met on a Sierra Club hike and lived out their lives in Yosemite Valley where they studied birds and flowers of the region. When you gaze at the Minarets from the east, Michael Minaret hovers slightly behind the main range like a gawky, uneasy visitor who isn't sure he has been invited to the party.

The entire area is chock-full of inspiring sights with extraordinary vistas in every direction. The blue waters of the aforementioned Ediza Lake contrast with the red and green deposits in the surrounding bluffs. Higher and closer to the range, Lower and Upper Iceberg Lakes are dominated by the gray granite cliffs shooting precariously above their shores. A large hemlock forest grows nearby, adding its "floppy tops" to the palate of natural beauty as though nodding in approval at what the artist has wrought.

᠎᠎᠎᠎᠎᠎᠎᠎᠎᠎᠎᠎᠎᠎᠎᠎᠎᠎᠎᠎᠎᠎᠎᠎᠎᠎᠎᠎᠎᠎᠎᠎᠎

Back at Ediza Lake in 1933, signs indicated that Peter had left for a day hike, traveling light, leaving behind his tent, crampons, and ice axe. This led some of the party to conclude that he had not intended to venture into the higher elevations, but Dawson had a different take on it and wrote in a letter, "It only made me believe that he was out to do real rock work." From Peter's campsite, a wide range of summits were within range, and only six of them had been previously climbed.

The searchers divided into the mountaineers and the nonmountaineers who would search the lower slopes and the trails leading up to the base of the range. The experienced climbers organized into four groups with different assignments: two climbers from Mammoth Lakes would summit Ritter, Peter's father and brother would search Banner, Clyde and a companion would climb Clyde Minaret, and Dawson and Eichorn would cross to the other side and investigate Michael Minaret. They set out at first light on August 16.

The two local climbers discovered that Peter had summited Ritter on July 30 and left a record in the register indicating that he had crossed the glacier from Ediza Lake using crampons and the ice axe. Notes from his ascent found at his camp, along with shots of the glacier on his camera, confirmed that information, and the fact that the equipment was back in camp made it reasonable to assume he had returned home safely that evening.

During their search, it must have preyed on the minds of Peter's father and brother that they had lost nine days since the planned rendezvous. Neither of the two had ever climbed Banner before, but of the four peaks, it was the least challenging—although given the context, that didn't mean much. They succeeded in reaching the top, but Peter had not signed the register, and they uncovered no clues as to his whereabouts.

Clyde and his fellow searcher scrambled across the glacier at the base of Clyde Minaret and advanced up the spire on its precipitous north face. Reaching the top, they determined that Peter had not signed the register. They would have liked to look around more carefully, but a thunderstorm was rapidly approaching, and neither wanted to be caught on top with lightning bolts striking all around. On the way down, zigzagging back and forth and looking for signs of Peter, they came across a set of "ducks"; a duck is a small stack of three rocks set by ascending mountain climbers to help them find the path back down. Further along, close to Upper Iceberg Lake, they discovered a bloody scrap of handkerchief of the type that Peter used. Those two clues would encourage Clyde to focus on Clyde Minaret, wrongly as it happened.

Meanwhile, Dawson and Eichorn had traveled through the notch, now known as Michael's Notch, that the Michaels had used to access the west side of the Minarets. They ascended one spire, thinking it was Leonard Minaret. When it was later discovered that they were the first to climb this particular peak, it would be named Dawson Minaret. Using a new chute, they climbed to the top of Michael Minaret and examining the register, realized that no one had signed since their entry two years earlier. Descending by a different chute, they came across a set of recent ducks and a half-smoked cigarette that would also turn out to be of the brand that Peter smoked. With storm clouds moving in and encircling the peak, they returned quickly to camp.

That evening back at camp, there was considerable speculation that Peter had fallen from Clyde Minaret into a bergschrund, the gap that opens when a glacier pulls away from snow adhering to a rock wall. This terrifying crevasse acts as a powerful, silent blender in which rocks, boulders and anything else that falls in are ground to bits by the action of the sliding, melting glacier. Depending on conditions and the size of the gap, traversing a bergschrund can present an enormous challenge to an alpinist. That would explain the signs of Peter in the vicinity and why his body appeared to have vanished.

On August 17, Clyde returned to Clyde Minaret but found only more mysterious ducks. Dawson and Eichorn summited Eichorn Minaret, but there was no entry from Peter in the register. They then explored several sides of Michael Minaret, including a valley between Michael and Clyde. They too found nothing new. By the time they returned that evening, the nonmountaineers had pulled out, convinced they had missed nothing in the lower portions of the search area.

Following further discussion, the group decided to scour the east side of Banner in case Peter had been drawn by a rarely used route up its face. But on August 18, those efforts were fruitless; by that evening, the discouraged team's talk turned to calling off the search. Clyde disagreed. He knew there were many cracks, ledges, crooks, and crannies that had not been investigated, and Peter could easily be hiding in one of those. The others didn't disagree but argued that any hope of finding him alive was gone. Peter's father and his brother needed to return home to be with Peter's mother in her time of grief. Clyde argued his case, but he was outvoted. The rest of the team departed. Clyde stayed behind.

Peter wasn't the only one to have friends with planes. After the CHP training effort using a helicopter to search for Matt came up empty, a climber who owned an old piper airplane mounted it with a RED digital camera, a high-tech camera used in the film industry, and flew it around the area. He and another of Matt Greene's friends shot over one hundred gigabytes of high definition video and then undertook the onerous task of analyzing the data, looking for anomalies. Matt's sister, Tiffany, hired SkyTime Helicopter Tours who sent a pilot and chopper out to search the area, but after two fruitless missions, she couldn't afford for them to keep looking.

Jill, John, and several of Greene's friends and fellow colleagues gathered in California and canvassed bus drivers, store owners, librarians, and others in Mammoth Lakes, posting flyers at trailheads. With no official SAR effort, a team of Matt's mountaineering colleagues arrived in town on August 10 and began working in the back country looking for clues. A searcher from SAR sent a message to the family, urging caution: "Anyone helping needs to understand that this is serious terrain. The altitude alone will do in many people. Just being a willing searcher who loves Matt is not enough. Anyone going into the backcountry needs to be skilled at handling the rigors of the mountains, otherwise there is risk of them becoming a victim as well."

Some local SAR personnel volunteered their time, and SWS Mountain Guides, a commercial guiding company, notified the family that they had climbed Clyde Minaret, the glacier route on Ritter, the north face of Ritter, the Ritter-Banner Saddle, the north ridge, and the south face of Banner. From all those efforts, nothing useful emerged.

By now, over twelve thousand people had "liked" Tiffany's Facebook page, and it had been "shared" by a multitude of people. It had attracted hundreds of comments, some useful like Greg Rutter's who wrote, "I am going up Clyde Minaret via Rock Route, will check that area."

Some were more eye-brow raising: "I am a psychic medium living in Australia and have been asked to help find Matthew. I feel he is underground or in a cave after falling and hurting his ankle."

Trudi wrote, "What if a wild.animal [sic] got him."

Dennis suggested, "Try checking the rivers."

Dan W. Ober opined, "What most likely happened is that he stopped to help someone and they turned on him."

Another wrote: "My worry is he may have stumbled upon a drug smuggling operation and was 'silenced.'"

Most just posted "prayers" or "I shared this."

At its first football game, Matt's high school decided to adopt a different hue from its ordinary blue and white, and the stands were a sea of "greene" for Matt. Senior Richard Gazzola told a Lehigh Valley news outlet, "I hope his family just realizes how much he's touched everyone here."

On Facebook, the students and teachers continued to sing Matt's praises. One student recounted a time when Matt stopped the class so he could scrape some gum off her desk that was bothering her. Another said that Matt was her favorite Math teacher and she was checking the Facebook page "what feels like 100 times a day hoping to see good news."

Tiffany posted another letter excerpt from Matt's time working with troubled youths in Colorado in 1998.

Breaking up over a dozen fights... repairing broken windows... watching a student dump an entire trash can over his teacher's head... hearing a class full of students call an enormous cop "pig" and tell him "get out—you don't belong here and we don't want to listen to you"... having the school director twice in one week make me physically remove three students from the building and lock the doors and bar the windows so they can't get back in. I'll miss working for youth benefits in Colorado. They seemed crazy until I realized where they come from. I grew up with Little League, soccer, track, fishing trips with Dad, meals with Mom, etc. These kids grew up wondering why Mom hasn't called in six years or why is she living in a shelter, why is Dad in jail, etc.

Understanding their roots is what allowed me to get through to them. Having them respect me enough to not curse at me or throw things at me like they did to everyone else was one of the biggest victories of my life. I learned a lot through that job, and now feel that if I get along with them, I can get along with anyone.

❦

Norman Clyde was old school. With his burly, powerful body, fierce wide-spaced eyes gazing evenly out of a craggy, square face, broad-brimmed hat jammed on his head, and ever-present ice axe, he looked as though he had emerged out of a stone cliff carved entirely in granite. While others were mountaineers, he *was* mountaineering. He was the most acclaimed climber in Sierra history. By 1933, he had made eighty-two first ascents, an almost inconceivable number. He stayed in the back country full time, moving from camp to camp in the summer and living in a caretaker's cabin in the winter. He earned a very frugal living as a guide or by writing articles.

He had not always been alone. He married in 1915 but lost his wife to tuberculosis only four years later. In 1924, following graduate studies at the University of California, Berkeley, he took a job as a teacher and the principal of the high school in Independence. On Halloween in 1928, he became aware of some "tricks" the students were planning to play at the school. He hid on the grounds, and when the kids appeared, he fired shots to scare them off. Appalled, the parents tried to have him arrested for attempted murder. They were unsuccessful, but the controversy forced his resignation. He would never hold a full-time job again.

After the rest of the search team departed, Clyde considered his options. He wrote later that he believed "it would afford a good deal of consolation to [Peter's] parents to know what had happened to him, particularly to be certain that he had not died a lingering death." Others would say that Clyde was just stubborn.

About that time, a tantalizing telegram dated August 18 was transmitted to him. A Sierra Club member wrote that he had encountered Peter on August 2 near Ediza Lake and that during their conversation, Peter had stated that he intended to bivouac by the Iceberg Lakes that night and would climb "North Minaret" the next day. This information would be extremely useful to Clyde as he continued the search. The only problem was—there is no "North Minaret." The Sierra Club member was not familiar with the Minarets and probably misunderstood Peter. Now Clyde was left in the position of puzzling over what a man he had never met might have said, using the words "north" or "northern," as a clue about his intentions for August 3.

On August 19, Clyde continued searching. His notes for the day read, "Went up to ridge north of Iceberg Lake leading westward toward what appeared to be Leonard Minaret, followed ridge westward across a glacier north to a wide 'U' notch; passed through notch and skirted base of Minarets on west side until abreast of Michael's Notch through which I passed and returned to camp." It reads like a precursor to the way Californians would be mocked on Saturday Night Live for elaborately describing the route they took to get somewhere: "I crossed the 5 and hitched a ride down to where 101 meets the 10, hung a right on El Hambre and got off at Sunset." Clyde did take note of the steep northwest face of Michael Minaret, remarking to himself, "capital place for a fall."

Over the next few days, Clyde would continue to summit other peaks, search in the canyons between the Minarets, and rest between climbing days. He returned again and again to Clyde Minaret where the inconclusive ducks tormented him. After scrutinizing the bergschrund, he decided that the lack of debris on the surface of the glacier was an indication that Peter had not fallen there.

Meanwhile, back in San Francisco, Peter's family was suffering from a lack of closure. His mother, in particular, was traumatized. In the face of no new information from the mountains, they decided to schedule a memorial service for Peter on Sunday, August 27.

On the previous Friday, Clyde decided to focus on Eichorn and Michael Minarets, where the cigarette butt and another line of ducks had been found. Their summits had been searched by Eichorn and Dawson, but there were many faces and chutes that remained unexplored. He started up the intimidating northwest face of Michael, but turned back and chose a different route to the summit, declaring the face too dangerous. Like Eichorn and Dawson, he found nothing at the top. Upon descending, he continued to scan the northwest face with binoculars although many areas were hidden. A storm was brewing, and he was forced to hurry. Following a ledge around a corner, he turned his binoculars back to the northwest face and discovered Peter's body lying on a ledge fifty yards away. He was dressed in a white T-shirt that contrasted sharply with the dark rock. He had fallen on his back and was gazing skyward, with his arms flung out.

༄

Eighty years later to the day from when Norman Clyde found Peter Starr's body, another search and rescue expert was looking for a missing climber he too had never met. Eastern Sierra local Dean

Rosnau had been exploring the back country for thirty-nine years and had participated in more than seven hundred SAR missions. After reading about Matt Greene's disappearance, he told the *Sheet*, "It would have haunted me, with my skills and my background if I didn't do something."

He had searched unsuccessfully on a previous outing, but continued to be pulled to the Ritter Range. He wrote on a climbing website, "I felt a strong leaning towards the Ritter/Banner theory. Frankly, it's what I would have done had I been in Matthew's position of wanting a fun, full value day in the mountains." On July 17, it was among the few areas that still had snow and ice and would have been within Matt's reach from Shady Rest Campground if he took the shuttle or caught a ride to Reds Meadow. Because of the text at 3:00 a.m., some believed that he might have started out very early that morning. And then there were the missing pages from his guidebook. Even with that focus, however, Rosnau said that one hundred professional searchers could spend the rest of their lives looking in the two hundred thousand acres of the Ansel Adams Wilderness and never find him.

On this day, he was accompanied by "Cupcake," described by Rosnau as a long-time friend, climbing partner, and "all around nut job." They were bent on navigating the Minaret Glacier, the icy slick on the east side of the range, terrain in Rosnau's words that is "as dangerous as it gets." A pair of glasses similar to Matt's had been found on a sign near Inyo Craters; Rosnau was anxious to hear if they matched Matt's prescription before he set out, but as of Sunday morning, it was still unknown if they were his.

That day, he and Cupcake entered at Agnew Meadows and hiked up to Ediza Lake along Shadow Creek with the intention of exploring the talus (the rocky slope at the base of a cliff) and the cliffs and chutes below the glacier. By noon, they had reached Iceberg Lake, had lunch, and then pressed on toward the glacier. The morning wind had turned into a full-force gale, affecting their footing as they ventured onto the talus below the glacier. After planning their strategy for the next day, they returned to camp where the wind had now risen to such a scream that they wore ear plugs during the night.

Before setting out on Monday, Rosnau radioed back from their base camp at Iceberg Lake and confirmed that the glasses were not Matt's. He and Cupcake then began the steep ascent to search the entire face below the toe of the glacier to look for signs that Matt might have fallen into the bergschrund, as was speculated, or had fallen onto the glacier and slid down its hard, slick surface. The cliff band was covered with heart-stopping drop-offs into deep slashes at the bottom of which roared the torrents of glacier runoff—freezing, racing waters waiting hungrily for anything or anyone to fall into their crushing stew. If the water doesn't get you, the slippery talus field lies at the ready, where any misstep can break an ankle or dislodge a cascade of boulders as big as refrigerators down the cliffs, carrying away anything in its path.

They continued up to the main part of the glacier just below Michael Minaret until they reached the maw, the lowest point of the glacier where the melting snow pours from its mouth. Rosnau described it as eight feet tall and reported that the glacier was groaning like a rusty hinge. "Spooky!" he wrote in his field notes. They carefully traversed several nearby chutes covered with slippery rubble and so steep that a loss of footing would result in a fall of hundreds of feet. One large gully rushing with ice water would serve as a funnel for anything rolling down off the glacier, including the visible boulders stuck above in the melting snow. Rosnau knew he had to check out the ledges below but also knew that he could not stay long; he would be tempting fate the entire time he was situated there below the glacier. After satisfying himself that there was nothing to find, he quickly snapped a selfie before getting the heck out of there.

Rosnau's photos convincingly convey the difficulty of the search, not only because of the danger to the searchers but also because of the hundreds of hard-to-search hiding places. At the end of the second day, having unearthed no new clues, Rosnau's feet dragged as he regretfully turned back toward Agnew Meadows to face the disappointment that his news would bring to Matt's family. Apart from a small white glove that was clearly not Matt's, they had uncovered no new signs. He addressed Matt in his search notes, "I feel a sense of the burden on your family and friends, how desperately they miss you and would like to know the answers to all their questions. Oh how it pains me to not be able to have those answers for them."

∽

After discovering Peter's body, Clyde immediately descended, hiked to Agnew Meadows, drove to Mammoth Lakes, and telegraphed the news to Walter Starr. The family discussed various options, but ultimately Starr telegraphed back to Clyde, "Do not try to remove remains." The memorial service took place as planned; upon arriving, guests filed past an enlargement of the last photo on Peter's camera, a beautiful landscape shot of Ediza Lake and the Minarets.

Several days later, a small group of mountaineers reconvened at the base of Michael Minaret with the plan to inter Peter's body where it lay. Jules Eichorn joined to assist, and he and Clyde entered the gully now known at Starr's Chute and carefully made their way across the treacherous north face. Then, roped together, they climbed straight up to Peter's ledge, a narrow, steep surface, with little room to maneuver. Near the body, they found Peter's pocket watch, smashed. It had stopped at 4:23. There were no other personal effects, such as his knapsack or hat.

Clyde turned out to be unwilling to touch the body, so twenty-one-year-old Eichorn dragged the body to a crack in the cliff wall and inserted it as well as he could, then covered it with rocks. It took him several hours to do this, and he reported that Clyde wept during the process. Eichorn himself was dismayed that he and Dawson had not discovered the body during their searching, as he felt it must have been visible, but the rock climbing in that area was highly technical, and they were most likely concerned with securing hand and foot holds.

Peter's father wrote in a letter to Dawson, "Clyde and Jules were able to entomb him against the wall, on the ledge. That is as it should be. He has become a part of one of the Sierra peaks he loved." At 12,000 feet, Peter's grave is the highest in the Sierra and perhaps in North America.

In 1936, the Sierra Club adopted a resolution to name a mountain near Mono Pass "Mount Starr" in Peter's honor. And in 1938, Walter Starr financed the publication of Ansel Adams' stunning photographs of the high country called *The Sierra Nevada and the John Muir Trail*. It was dedicated to Peter, and Walter Starr used it to persuade Congress to designate Kings Canyon as a national park.

Peter's notes on the region were posthumously compiled and published as Starr's Guide *to the John Muir Trail and the High Sierra Region*. Now in its twelfth edition, it remains an important resource for hikers and climbers. Of it, his father wrote, "May the traveler feel the companionship of that eager, joyous, and generous youth who loved the beauty of the mountains and wanted others to share his love."

c. 9

In 2014, Matt's dad, Bob, traveled to Mammoth Lakes to undertake a rigorous one-man search over the course of the summer. From Pennsylvania, he had initiated an email correspondence with Rosnau who was initially opposed to this endeavor and wrote later he threw "everything at him" to try to talk him out of it. He emphasized the likelihood that an out-of-shape sixty-seven-year-old would get into trouble in such dangerous terrain at altitude and the unlikelihood that he would find anything. He did not anticipate the determination of a grieving father looking for his missing son. Unwavering, Bob began training with a forty-five-pound pack, going for long hikes around the wintery Pennsylvania countryside, including local areas of the Appalachian Trail. He lost weight, bought gear, and arranged for a condo. He was, in Rosnau's words, "a man with a mission."

Arriving in Mammoth Lakes in May, he began with conditioning front-country hikes while he waited impatiently for the snow pack to melt enough to allow him access into the Minarets. He uploaded detailed notes of his daily solitary outings to a trekking website, including commentary on the difficulty of the terrain and recommendations for family-friendly trails. His pleasure in discovering the deer, grouse, quail, coyotes, and fish of the Eastern Sierra is evident, and as a dam expert, he was impressed by the construction efforts to build the Agnew Lake and Gem Lake Dams. On May 18, he hiked over Mammoth Pass down to Reds Meadow and back, a tough

1,800 foot ascent on the return. From the top of the pass, he could see the tantalizing but still snow-locked Minarets in the distance. When the road down to Reds Meadow opened at the end of May, he immediately began descending to evaluate the snowpack around Ediza Lake and Thousand Island Lake. It was still thick.

By June, he was camping in the backcountry, spending his days searching the base of the cliffs of the Ritter Range and glassing the upper areas up to the snow line. He emerged every three to five days to reprovision. He wore a SPOT locator, an electronic device that uploaded his geographic coordinates, and his family tracked his movements every day. The data was further loaded into findmespot. com to mark the areas he had searched. By June 30, he had found no sign of Matt. "Another blade of hay has been eliminated from the stack," he wrote at the end of long day, "but the search for the needle continues."

Partway through his initiative, he received an exciting visit from Detective Hornbeck. Two hikers who had been in Mammoth Lakes the year before had come back to town. They spotted the flyers about Matt and came forward to report that they had camped next to him at Shady Rest. They were somewhat unsure about what day they had talked to him, but they were certain he had said that he was headed to the Minarets. The news intensified Bob's focus on the area.

For the first three days in July, Rosnau joined him, and the two headed back to the Minaret Glacier. By then, Bob had logged over four hundred miles in the Eastern Sierra and was a toughened, mos- quito-bitten, hard-core hiker. After setting out from Agnew Meadows a little before 6:00 a.m., to test Bob's stamina, Rosnau set a brutal pace up to Iceberg Lake where they would set up base camp at the same site that he and Cupcake had used. According to the proud

Rosnau, Bob stayed right with him. According to the more modest Bob, Rosnau "pretty much blew me away."

Portions of the area that Rosnau had hoped to search were still snow-covered, so he ascended a cliff face leading to Cecile Lake that is next to the terrible gully that he and Cupcake had searched. Partway up, he made a stunning discovery—a water bottle in a carrying pouch that showed appropriate wear for having passed the winter there. Yelling for Bob, he continued to search for other clues and shortly thereafter found a pocket knife that had surely been exposed for years. Rosnau quickly snapped photos of the items, and the two climbed higher in search of a cell signal. With the assistance of his pals on supertopo.com, the photos were loaded onto the site for potential identification purposes. Rosnau was beside himself with excitement. If those items belonged to Matt, the men could be quite close to their target.

Meanwhile, the day had gotten very hot, and the two searchers rested in the shade of a tree to catch their breath before they noticed some ominous clouds were gathering overhead. Hurrying down to pump some water, they then set off back down the slippery rocks to Iceberg Lake while lightning and thunder began to abuse the cirque above them. After a big meal back in camp, they fell asleep to the sound of rain.

The next day was clear, and the two prepared themselves for an arduous day. Rosnau's plan was to ascend to the glacier, but then instead of searching to the south as he and Cupcake had done, he and Bob would turn right and investigate to the north under Dawson Minaret. When they reached the glacier, they stopped for lunch and an Internet break and learned that the water bottle and knife were not Matt's. Disappointed but tenacious, they picked their way through the talus and boulder fields to the bottom of Dawson Minaret and explored a snow-packed chute, rushing with ice water, where they discovered an incongruous mylar balloon under a rock overhang. Balloon in tow, they carefully descended to the moraine below, heading back to camp to conclude their day with dinner and conversation.

Over the past two days, Rosnau and Bob had gotten to know each other and, connected by tragedy, had forged a friendship. Rosnau was cultivating a deep respect for Bob and his considerable and ongoing efforts to find his son. Knowing the father and seeing what a great influence he must have been on his son made Rosnau all the more frustrated that he had never met Matt and that he could not find him now. On the morrow, on his way out after another day of failure, Rosnau again cried out to Matt, "Damn, you are hard to find! I feel as though I know you so much better now that I have met the amazing man who raised you. I'm sure you're looking down on him with pride. He fits in here, Matthew. The mountains that spoke to your soul now do to his."

Bob then met up with five of Matt's friends, fellow teachers who flew in from Pennsylvania to help with the search. They climbed Clyde Minaret and investigated the south notch glacier and around Cecile Lake, taking a day off to do some catch-and-release trout fishing in Skelton Lake before returning to Riegelhuth Minaret, the talus area south of Minaret Lake, and the gullies up to the crest. Besides encountering a black bear, they did not uncover anything unexpected. Bob also took a break to kindly escort several of the teachers on a sight-seeing trip to Devils Postpile and Rainbow Falls.

Tiffany and her mother came out on July 12 to be there for the one-year anniversary of Matt's disappearance. Together with Matt's friends, they spent a few days taking in the scenery, checking out the Pacific Crest Trail, and climbing up to Crystal Crag for an up-close look at the kind of technical climbing Matt was fond of. On July 17, they placed new flyers, now including pictures of the gear that Matt had been carrying, and hiked to Ediza Lake to look at the search area. Tiffany described it as "stunning." "Matt is with us in spirit," she wrote on Facebook and posted a spectacular photo of the lake. Though she enjoyed the unusual vistas, she was crushed to return home several days later after finding nothing new. They had been so hopeful. "Hard to turn around," she wrote, "knowing he's out there." Waiting for her red eye home on July 19, she cried for the first time all week.

The summer wore on. Bob returned to the Minarets, hoping to access the west side but couldn't find a pass he felt he could safely solo. He elected to search the area between Deadhorse Lake and Ediza Lake and the talus slopes north of Cecile Lake up to the Gap. "The search was very slow going due to the vast rockfalls and steep slopes that need to be examined," he wrote. "Even with due diligence, many, many areas were missed." On Bob's July 26 birthday, his thoughts must have turned to the signed, sealed, and stamped card his son had left behind in his car when he disappeared the year before, ready to be mailed in time for his father's 2013 birthday.

On August 1, Bob was determined to make it to the west side, and climbed the rigorous 3,000 feet from Agnew Meadows to north Glacier Pass. Exhausted after a seven-hour climb, he tucked into his tent out of the wind but within earshot of the rocks falling off the Ritter and Banner peaks. The next day he finally attained the west side and searched and glassed the region around the Ritter Lakes, and on the third day, after some navigation difficulties, he descended to

Hemlock Crossing and on to Headquarters Meadows. On August 4, it was back to Reds Meadow and a shuttle ride to Agnew Meadows, his starting place. No sign of Matt.

On August 12, Bob decided to check out two of the approach routes to Mount Ritter that were included in the pages that Matt had torn from his guidebook. Arriving at the bottom of the southeast glacier, he looked up the chute that rose 300 feet to the ridge and paused, encountering another climber who doubted his abilities to summit and was waiting for his friends who had left him behind three-and-a-half hours earlier. Bob waited for the hiker's friends who returned within thirty minutes and then descended with them until he broke off to investigate an alternate version of the path up to the top. It was a strenuous day, and Bob noted that his legs were cramping that night.

A few days later, Bob decided again to attack Mount Ritter via a more moderate chute than the one he had gazed up the week before. He described this approach as more boulder hopping and rock negotiating than technical climbing. He did find a water filter embedded in the upper glacier ice, but Matt's was already accounted for. He summited on August 19 and left a message for his son in the register and returned to Agnew Meadows the next day.

On his last two days, Bob explored again on the east side of the Minarets. On the first day, he climbed in the area around Deadhorse Lake, including a side trip to find the abandoned Minaret Mine down in the valley where Steve Fossett, the adventurer pilot, crashed in 2007. On the second day, Bob summited Pridham Minaret, leaving another message for his son in the register, noting that his message now lies at both ends of the Ritter Range, the area he describes as "most likely to be Matt's final resting place."

Thus ended Bob's four-month sojourn into the wild to search for Matt. He had hiked over six hundred fifty miles and grown close to the achingly beautiful but heartless landscape that had captured his son. He had made a friend and grown wiser and stronger, but the conclusion was ultimately unsatisfying. Tiffany wrote on Facebook, "'The Mountains are calling...'—that resonates."

In recounting these parallel tragedies, the writer is obliged to recognize that, no matter her compassion and sympathy, her words will fail to fully render the tourbillion of emotions suffered by the friends and families of the missing. Indeed they themselves recognize that however useful words are for everyday living, there are times when they forsake us.

Peter's mother wrote in a letter to Clyde, "I know of no words adequate in which to express to you the gratitude I feel for your great efforts which finally resulted in your finding our beloved boy."

In late 2013, one of Tiffany's Facebook posts read, "Braving the cold, a neck injury, and some of the most dangerous terrain in the world, [Rosnau] has sacrificed his time, health, job and family to aid us and push us forward. There are no words to express our thanks, our frustrations, our sadness and our hope."

In early 2015, another climber, haunted by the events surrounding Matt's disappearance, dreamed of bringing solace to the Greene family. As a moderator of the High Sierra Topix mountaineering website, Maverick could access the most talented of its subscribers and began organizing an effort to return to the Ritter Range and scour it with a group of volunteers. By March, a large number of experienced climbers had expressed interest in participating, and SAR experts, some with forty years of experience, were working with Maverick on an investigation into what had happened. Despite never having met Matt, Maverick told me in an interview, "I want to do this for a fellow mountaineering brother. Our passion for the mountains binds us all together." The group set plans to return just after Labor Day 2015.

On September 9, the group convened in Mammoth Lakes and set up camp at Shady Rest. The next day, they tried to retrace Matt's footsteps with what little information they had. They stopped by McDonalds in the morning as had been Matt's habit and couldn't help but think about what clues could have been discovered if the security footage had been checked. "It definitely has your mind going," Maverick said.

By September 11, they had set up at Ediza Lake, as many had before them, and were in the backcountry, checking the boulder and talus fields around Southeast Glacier and the Clyde Variation. The group was surprised to discover how much usage the area gets, raising the question about why Matt had not yet been found and how hidden he might be. On the other hand, Maverick noted that their search was not even close to 100 percent, and that until one is actually on site, it's hard to imagine the size and complexity of the terrain and how easily a body could disappear.

On Saturday, September 12, the group split up with most going to the Ritter-Banner saddle while Maverick headed up beyond Deadhorse Lake to check the fall zones under Kehrlein Minaret. He had a hunch that if Matt was exploring on the southern side of Kehrlein and had lost his footing, he would have fallen away from the cliff and ended up in a certain concealed ravine. It wasn't just a hunch that led him to the area. Several clairvoyants had independently indicated that area was of interest, and while Maverick was skeptical, he commented that it was too big of a coincidence to ignore. "Sometimes they're right," he said.

Arriving at a chute that led to the ravine, he discovered that indeed if someone fell in there, he would be completely blocked from view. He also discovered a ledge system that called out to be investigated, but it would require rappelling gear to do so. Studying the area, he suddenly became aware of the wind picking up and clouds moving in and realized he had to get out of there quickly before the oncoming storm.

After hurrying back to camp, he rejoined the rest of the crew who had found nothing new during their day of searching and were discouraged by the smoke in the air from a wildfire on the west side of the Sierra. It was tempting to get frustrated by their lack of progress, but Maverick counseled the group to channel that emotion into increased focus and more positivity. "Besides," he said, "it's wonderful to see people out there looking, trying to get some closure for the family."

The next day, the group again thoroughly explored the cross-country hike from Ediza to Iceberg to Cecile to Minaret Lakes to check that popular and appealing area off their list since Matt had expressed interest in it. By afternoon, clouds had again moved in, and it began raining hard at Ediza Lake, flooding the meadow where the searchers were camped. Reading the weather, they conferred and decided to pack up and head out rather than risk getting themselves and all their gear soaked. It was time to go. On the way out, looking back, they could see snow on the Minarets. Their search was over.

But only for now. Maverick explained that exploring the rough country was eye-opening. "With the landslides and the glaciers constantly moving, things can quickly disappear and reappear. The landscape has a life of its own, so evidence can be swallowed up or spit back out." He suggested that an El Niño year could bring new things to light.

Meanwhile, his postings on the climbing sites were driving a theory that Matt might have intended to summit Kehrlein Minaret and traverse over to Starr, a Minaret named for Peter Starr's father when he summited the peak in 1937 on an outing with Ansel Adams to honor Peter's memory. This potential route would open up a different area of focus for a search group, and one that had not been explored. Speculation, information, and high fives continue to mount on the threads devoted to Matt's disappearance, and postings and views on supertopo.com exceeded twenty-three thousand. Fellow climbers continued to try to put themselves in the mind of a thoughtful, experienced adventurer and collectively puzzle over what it meant that Matt had taken crampons and an ice axe, but no helmet. Plans already started forming for searchers to return again in 2016, possibly with the assistance of an expert drone pilot. Maverick wrote, "In no way has the search for Matthew concluded. His love for these mountains is a beacon for all others."

༄

While learning about Peter and Matt, I was struck by the remarkable similarities of their stories, not only in the coincidental facts and details, but also in the personalities behind them—the strong character of each man, his independence, and his passionate attachment to the Sierra. Matt was contemplating the tensions between passion and reason while he was reading W. Somerset Maugham's *Of Human Bondage*. He wrote to a friend, "Why do we sit back and allow reason to crush the passion in us as we age? I don't know why our minds always gravitate to reason. It's a nuisance. It's a pitiful thing when people reach the point in their lives when passionate inclinations no longer win out over regular routine." I suspect that Peter would have agreed. Only a few days before his death, he wrote a poem entitled *The Mountain's Call* that concluded with the lines, "Defiant mountains beckon me, To glory and dream in their paradise." Matt's and Peter's stories color in the picture of two men who heeded that beckoning and whose love for the mountains led ultimately to their demise.

The stories also reveal what unites those who are driven to find their brethren when they go missing. The searchers, the *indagans*, are haunted by the missing, the *absens*, and go to great effort even at personal risk to discover the answer to the question that I asked on the shuttle: *What happened?* Even after hope for a rescue has winked out, they continue to look, hoping to find resolution for the families of the missing and for themselves. After the tragic death of adventurers, we attempt to temper grief with the clichéd adage that "at least they died doing what they loved." The plight of the searchers teaches us what cold comfort that dispassionate reckoning offers. Unable to move on, the searchers persist—determined to reach the end of the story, to uncover what happened to someone who played the odds and lost, and perhaps to gain insight into their own mortality.

LANDSCRAPS

The gauntlet: Lone Pine Independence   Big Pine Bishop
Hurry
Big business, bright lights, shiny dollar
car car   van   SUV car   SUV   SUV
north to snow-condo-hot tub

Then the ground opens
                    A chasm churned by water
                              Scars parched and silent
          Testaments to a violent past

          That desperate Scrabble word of last resort: aa

A brief patch of green
that looks right
lush with valley life
sheep and cattle graze

Back
                    to the geological and ecological assault!
          Foothills writhe   struggle under the strangling grip

a four-year drought   A hand
    doles out tortuous drops of water
A twisted tree raises a supplicant   f

    i

    n

    g

    e

    r   to the skies

    in hope of salvation

    or a quicker death

    aa   aa

Electric wires   m a r c h   across the dustbowl
    Waterways

    carved into its flesh

    whisk away the land's Chi

    feed the monster in the south

    like the Matrix machines

    that huffed and wheezed over the humans

    Sucked away their life energy

to sustain the devil's snare   dystopian civilization

Darkness falls
the Sierra wave   perches off the ridge
like a patch of crimson hounds,
    sticking   their heads out the car windows

    their tongues and ears stream back in the wind

    lava   aa   tephra

The grooves in ancient foothills   are hopelessly bone dry
     Much   higher
                   snow appears
A sprinkling of powdered sugar   on the highest peaks
      of a scrambled   chocolate pudding cake

     Abandoned   buildings
stumble   across the landscape   or   c-o-l-l-a-p-s-e
   hollow-eyed   next to the roadway

         Dilapidated hotels
         hunker under
    faded   vacancy   signs

twisting in the gritty   w   i   n   d
                          precarious
    survivors of decades of bad luck
       and the slimmest of political victories

     magma   pumice   aa

Stop-motion images of frozen gray chop
         LOOM
          in the distance
Lava detritus litters the ground
  Leftover blackened bolts
    from a fiery battle
     of the underground gods

A red cinder hill   rises   to block your path
A ribbed wall
            un~du~lates   over the ground
      Giant fungi   around the next bend
Lava creatures return
        horned and gnarled   c r a w l in g
        threaten and glare   spiky tails rise
                  heads sway
fight fight
          aa   aa

Illustration - Whitmore Soccer Field

GETTING SCHOOLED

I have no life. My kid plays sports.

~ Mammoth license plate frame

September 4–10, 2014

Thursday

Dave and Christine and Tom and I all accompanied Julian on his ride to school today. We have found yet another route, one that features three bike-only bridges and one tunnel. With our sunglasses and fluorescent safety jackets, we looked like a posse of bug-eyed aliens providing security for a middle schooler. Julian rode like a bat out of hell—maybe he was trying to get away from us. We hung around briefly to hear the morning school announcements and the most lugubrious pledge of allegiance I have ever heard. The boy who led the pledge sounded like he was suffering from major depression. Tom wondered hopefully if the effect was deliberate, a sly nose-thumbing.

A space has opened up on a soccer team, and Julian was pulled off the waiting list! His coach called this morning, and the first practice was this afternoon, AND there are games Saturday and Sunday. His coach, Alex, has a thick accent and was not particularly easy to understand on the phone. I was secretly thrilled as we hoped Julian would have more contact with Spanish when we moved here. And sure enough, instructions from the sidelines were primarily in Spanish.

We went to the Loco Frijole for dinner (I don't know why it's not the Frijole Loco—it seems as though it should be—a friend later points out that it should be Frijol, not Frijole). The waitress started with Julian, and he ordered in Spanish! She then turned to me but scolded me when I tried to order in English.

"Nah-ah," she said, *"En español."* So we all ordered in Spanish with varying levels of success.

As we were leaving for dinner, a UPS truck drove up and stopped at our driveway. It looked like a noisy, hulking brown apparition from another life. The driver handed Julian a small package containing his new baseball pants and rumbled off. I couldn't help wondering, *How far had it driven? Did it have any other deliveries in Mammoth? Surely it hadn't driven all the way up from Bishop (or further) just for baseball pants, right? Right?*

Friday

It has been very fun to show Christine all the bicycling infrastructure here, the trails and paths and bridges and tunnels, and how much bicycling has become part of the community, especially for the kids. Of the first soccer teammates who showed up to practice yesterday, five for five arrived by bicycle. And the sixth arrived on a skateboard. Bikes are all over the place at apartment complexes: on balconies, under stairs, piled next to front doors. Trails are well maintained and marked with extensive signage showing the network of trails, mile markers, and emergency information.

Christine is the education director for the bike coalition in Santa Barbara, a group that has been successfully working to make the city a friendly place to bike for over twenty-five years. Impressed with our bicycling culture, she took careful notes and photos to document the environment. We set out this morning to understand how all this came about and made some inquiries at the Mammoth Lakes Welcome Center and the Mammoth Lakes Tourism office.

As is often true in Mammoth, the story starts with an inspired individual, in this case, John Wentworth, a show business refugee who had worked as a co-producer on several David Lynch projects, including *Mulholland Drive* and *Twin Peaks: Fire Walk With Me*. John described his role in the trails project as one who lit a couple of sparks that grew into a perfect storm of opportunity.

The inciting incident occurred when conflict flared between backcountry skiers and aggrieved local residents with homes on Ranch Road on the edge of the Inyo National Forest. The skiers were accustomed to accessing the Sherwin Range via Ranch Road but found one day that their usual egress was being threatened by an enormous gate to be constructed by the residents on what had been a local public road. Wentworth was intrigued by the situation and the obvious need for some sort of public easement, recalling from his youth in New England several public paths that accessed the beaches. He and his associates recognized that large issues were at stake that could dramatically affect the future of the town. The community rallied and created the Mammoth Lakes Trails and Public Access Foundation, known locally as MLTPA.

MLTPA began working hard in 2006 to pull together interested parties to address various considerations: the relationship between the town and the public lands that surround it, the recreational appeal of the area, and how to better connect people and nature. It turned out that a lot of people were interested; when MLTPA hosted a public meeting and strategic planning conference, over three hundred people showed up. The seeds of a plan were laid out to connect new town trails with hundreds of miles of existing front country forest trails and the John Muir and Pacific Crest Trails. As planning progressed, representatives from multiple agencies, including the US Forest Service, the Town of Mammoth Lakes, Caltrans, and various conservancy groups participated in updating a comprehensive master plan for a four-season trails system. Upon completion, the trail system would provide coordinated access to the extraordinary natural areas in the Mammoth Lakes vicinity, such as Yosemite and Devils Postpile, and some of the most beautiful scenery in the American West. As Wentworth said, "It was a very big project."

The trails planning effort was initially funded by Mammoth Mountain Ski Area and the Town, who each committed $100,000, and MLTPA was awarded a grant from the newly established Sierra Nevada Conservancy. In subsequent years, two new tax measures, Measure R and Measure U, were approved by over two-thirds of Mammoth residents to invest in trails, recreation, parks, arts and culture, and mobility. The town also obtained federal grants to fund the building and construction of trails and bike paths. In all, it took about $20 million to bring the plan to fruition.

Incredibly, this partnership of multiple agencies was able to accomplish many of their goals in only six years following the strategic conference. In 2012, the town celebrated the opening of the Mammoth Lakes Trail System, including the flagship Lakes Basin Path, an awe-inspiring trail that goes all the way up to the Horseshoe Lake parking lot from the Village at Mammoth and includes at least two tunnels and numerous bridges. Unlike most infrastructure projects, especially those that involve bike paths, those accomplishments came together relatively quickly, and demonstrate what passionate people can achieve when supported by the public will. John Wentworth still lives in Mammoth Lakes and now serves on the Town Council.

Speaking of the Lakes Basin Path, Dave and Christine knocked off work early, and we scooted over on our bikes to the Lakes Basin trolley, which turns out to still be running in September. Tom rode down to accompany Julian from school and zipped up Main Street to catch the trolley. We loaded our bikes onto the trolley's trailer and boarded the trolley with a lean toughened guy in a blue jumpsuit who was carrying an oversize skateboard. He asked to go up only as far as Lake Mary.

"Gets kinda flat after that," he said and grinned.

It turns out his intention was to scream back down Lake Mary Road, apparently for fun. We quizzed him about his equipment and technique: he rides on his back with his neck supported by a Styrofoam headrest. I assumed he rode down the bike path, thinking that would be safer than rumbling down amongst the cars.

"Nah. Too many pine needles on the bike path," he said. "Makes you slip."

He said he rides feet first because "I'd rather break my foot than my head, ya know?"

When he gathered his equipment to get off, Tom said, "Oh, and you wear a helmet!"

The guy did a double take, then got it, and gave that goofy grin again, revealing what may or may not have been a set of capped teeth.

Our driver serves as a host on the mountain during the winter and loves to talk about Mammoth. I would say he has a hard time not talking in general. He told us about the caldera and the fumaroles (he did *not* tell about the three ski guides who died tragically one after another, trying to save each other, in the fumarole on the face of Chair 3 in 2006), about the carbon dioxide killing all the trees around Horseshoe Lake, how big a trout his friend caught last weekend, how he himself only practices catch and release, where the chapel is on Twin Lakes, and how long he's been married—and then he pointed out a deer in the woods. He also showed us Hole in the Wall, a rock face with a tunnel in it that the daredevils ski through in the winter. It looked terrifying, even without the snow.

A bit buffeted by all this information, we set off around Horseshoe Lake, and everyone had fun navigating the roots and rocks and egging each other on to do the jumps. We're definitely getting stronger. Julian whips up "Library Hill" now like it's nothing, and the climb up Main Street doesn't seem as daunting as it did. Julian even climbed up to the Lake George Lodge through all the switchbacks on his heavy bike with its small wheels. He and I took the quick descent home while the others biked the Panorama Dome Trail and met us back at home for roasted chicken and vegetables.

Saturday

Julian had a soccer game today and he has one tomorrow, both down at Whitmore. As if that wasn't enough driving, we forgot his shin guards and shoes and I had to abandon him there and drive pell-mell back to town, being careful not to kill any of the hundreds of Mammoth Fall Century bike racers riding up US 395 or get caught by the patrolling California deputies circling up and down the highway to keep people like me from speeding. I arrived back at the field one minute before the game started. It takes exactly fifteen minutes to drive from Whitmore to our house if you consistently drive the speed limit (or a teensy-weensy bit over).

The game was... well, lopsided. Julian's team is Yellow (apparently they're at the age where they're too cool to have an actual name), and the opposing Greenies looked tall and lanky in comparison. With Julian in goal, the opposition scored in the first ten seconds of the game, which set the tone. After the first quarter, they were up 4–0 and the rest of the game was downhill. There were very few whistles, unlike back home. The game was clean without the level of aggression that we used to see in Del Mar—not sure what to make of that.

Julian's PE teacher has created "Project A"; the kids must hike three trails in the area, either of their choice or from a list of qualifying trails, in order to get an A in the class. "Get out there and show your friends and parents this beautiful area we live in," says the teacher's page on the school website. He further advises the students to take a photo of themselves as evidence of completion.

Thank goodness the hike to Crystal Lake we did a couple weeks ago qualified or that trek would have just been a waste. Another qualifying hike is "up Convict Canyon." We had hiked around Convict Lake last year and wanted to show Dave and Christine the dramatic, multicolored cliffs above the lake. We all met up at Whitmore after they had ridden down with Tom on the gravel road from town. It's a long rough ride and just about shook Christine's teeth out of her head—she announced she was done with riding for the day when she arrived. So, we loaded their bikes onto the van and, after the game, drove over to Convict Lake.

The trail up the canyon branches off a trail we did last year and meanders in easy switchbacks up the rising meadow; it heads toward a ridge over which I hoped we would be able to see the creek that feeds the lake or maybe even a waterfall. It was not to be. We were losing light and energy and had to turn back after a mile or so. With the wizardry of modern technology, Dave had loaded the trail onto his phone and could show me how far it goes, up to a very high lake. Someday. We declared the distance that we had hiked as enough to qualify for Project A and took a photo as proof.

Sunday

In order to slip in one last hike, we drove up to the Panorama Dome trailhead before Dave and Christine had to head home and we had to set out for a day of soccer and baseball, soccer at Whitmore and baseball in Bishop. It was terrifically gusty at the top where you can look out over the town, peer down at Twin Lakes, or gaze at the waterfall off in the distance. The wind was really roiling down the waterfall canyon and stealing everyone's hats. We jumped around for a while and then had to return to real life.

After Yellow lost again at Whitmore, we headed down to Bishop for baseball. It wasn't the Bishop parents who beat us up—it was the kids! They didn't do it all at once. Mammoth scored in the first, and then Bishop tied it up and scored another run or two here and there and then really broke the thing open in the fourth inning when innumerable overthrows later, they were up some ungodly number of runs. Mammoth never recovered. Both teams looked raggedy and suffered from early-season errors.

Some of the Mammoth soccer insiders were sitting behind us whispering about the uneven soccer teams and the difficulty of evening them up by getting some good kids to switch to bad teams. One of them was half defending himself—apparently he was responsible for team allocation—by blaming the kids for not playing as well as they were supposed to, or, even worse, for playing a lot better than he thought they would. I suspect that Yellow is one of the "bad" teams, although they said something about Alex always finding a way to win. That would not surprise me. I think there's a lot of talent on that team, but he doesn't have kids playing in the right spots yet. I learned later that he had coached a championship team the year before that won one of the cup tournaments. When the soccer insiders had quit conspiring (without a conclusion) and had moved on to discuss how they might find a way to beat Bishop this year in soccer, I asked how the Mammoth athletes usually fared against Bishop.

"Well… not too good," said the team allocator.

"Why?" I asked guilelessly.

He looked a little surprised but then said, "Bigger population."

It's true that Bishop *feels* bigger because it has the Kmart and the rodeo, but according to Wikipedia, its population is only thirty-nine hundred compared to Mammoth's eighty-two hundred. Maybe it's hard to get a good census in a resort town with so many transients. And the Mammoth transients don't add much to your soccer or baseball teams. And Bishop might pull from the surrounding area, although I don't know what that does for you if no one lives there either.

"We beat 'em in skiing," the guy said, and we all laughed. I suspect that weather is a factor; the Bishop kids can play ball many more months of the year.

The newspaper had an article about the football "rivalry" between Bishop and Mammoth, although the writer admitted he used the word loosely because… ah, Mammoth has never won. There might have been some game back in the seventies that Mammoth won (perhaps it was played in a snow storm). The current coach also remembers a game he played in (he's a Mammoth High alum) in which Mammoth was up 26–7, but Bishop came back and won. Their first match of the season is next Friday, and the town does seem quite fired up about it.

In any case, the Bishop parents were friendly and didn't rub in their victory. Maybe they were too over-heated to be hard on us or felt sorry for the mountain folk suffering in the sweltering sunshine. It was incredibly hot, still in the nineties, even at 3:30 p.m. The wind was blowing hard, but it didn't seem to bring much relief. Fortunately, one of the baseball moms invited us under her umbrella or I honestly think we might have expired. We all breathed a sigh of relief when we tumbled out of the car at home into the cool darkness.

Monday

For the first time since we have arrived, there were clouds this morning; it sprinkled lightly this afternoon in a brief respite from our heat wave, which is forecast to return by Thursday.

A big bear was hit and killed on US 395 during the night. It caused a traffic jam in the morning as everyone slowed down to check out the poor bear. Tom has reminded me to be careful on my bike and watch out for deer and other wildlife. A squirrel did attempt suicide by running under my front tire, but I managed to shriek pointlessly and somehow foiled his effort.

As is appropriate for a town where soccer is taken very seriously (although I'm beginning to suspect, more seriously by the coaches than the kids), two-hour soccer practices are scheduled for Monday, Wednesday, and Thursday. With games on Saturday, that's a lot of soccer. Tom rode with Julian over to Shady Rest from school; I joined them later to watch practice, read and write, and bring Julian and his bike home in the car. As most of the kids arrive by bike, the other parents are nowhere to be seen.

Journalist Dave Barry wrote how youth sports had changed since he played. He had recently attended a soccer tournament and was astonished at how the parents SCREAMED at the kids. In his day, the kids got themselves to their baseball games on their bikes, and if a parent had shown up in the middle of the day to watch one of their games, they would have thought that person was *insane*. And now that's me.

Tuesday
In a depressing story, the dead body of a deranged young man from Nevada was found this weekend behind some condos. The investigation is still underway, but residents reported that they observed him hitting himself in the head with a fire extinguisher late that afternoon, although he had disappeared by the time medical help arrived. His body had been dragged during the night, authorities speculated, by either a bear or a mountain lion. They emphasized that the young man was already dead by the time his body was mauled. "I just don't want people to think there's an animal going around attacking people," one of them said.

Two coyotes trotted self-importantly across the bike path in front of us near Snowcreek as we rode home from school. They looked good: richly colored coats and bushy tails. They appeared to be headed toward Vons, perhaps for the sale on ground beef.

Tom and I spotted a large unusual raptor this morning along Meridian. It had a smooth round white head. Tom speculated that it was a hawk, and I do see that some Swainson's hawks have white heads and are considered fairly common in Mammoth. A more knowledgeable person suggested later that it was a bald eagle.

I also saw two brown-gray hen-looking ground birds on my hike on Old Mammoth Road. They looked like quail without the goofy little ball looping over their heads. They were quite pretty and friendly. I have a list of Mammoth Lakes birds, and after studying the Internet for an hour, I conclude they were blue grouses.

I was surprised to discover that I had neglected to bring any soccer socks. The local stores seem to ignore the sports needs of the residents—neither the Kmart nor the sports store next door carried any baseball gear—so I decided once again the Cast Off thrift store was my best bet. I hiked down there a few days ago and (hooray!) found a pair. Today I was very surprised to discover not two, not four, not six, but *seven* pairs of soccer socks in a drawer I hadn't checked. So, for any of you planning on visiting, we're good on soccer socks.

Wednesday

Trash day! Tom says such romantic things to me on trash day, like, "The momentum of my trash is carrying me up on top of you," when he accidentally overtakes me on the bike path. His child trailer filled with recycling bins rattled and clinked as it bumped over the rough spots on the bike trail.

"That is one noisy baby," I said.

"That's why I'm taking it to the dump," he retorted.

A woman at the transfer station said, "Well, that's cute," when Tom snapped off the trailer cover to expose his bags of sorted recycling. On the way home, a lady on the walking trail peered hopefully into the trailer and, observing that it was empty, looked up at me with a perplexed look. I didn't have time to explain about the trash.

The full moon has been beautiful at night. It's amazing how much light it makes, illuminating the whole street outside our house. And even on this sunny morning, it was huge and glowing over Mammoth Mountain as we turned to enter the transfer station.

Consistent with the not-quite-in-time aspect of soccer in Mammoth, the coach called this morning to say the Yellow team had a previously unannounced game this afternoon against the Red team that would partially conflict with baseball. Through a controversial trade, Yellow had gained a couple talented new players, and the team tied the game at three, but they couldn't overcome the mighty Red. Due to on-going mother incompetence, Julian had to play baseball in soccer shorts and cleats. No one seemed to mind, and the coaches were very gracious about him showing up an hour late with wrong gear. "Just show up, that's the thing," Chief said.

September 11–17, 2014
Thursday
On the way home from school, Tom took me on East Bear Lake Drive, a pristine modern two-lane road with gutters and sidewalks—and no houses. It's as though you can point to a line in the dirt and say, "Here is where the housing bubble popped." On West Bear Lake Drive, a long empty road eventually led to a cluster of spectacular grandiose houses, huddled together. All empty.

You know you live in a small town when you find out that the couch you've been eyeing at the thrift store has sold—by seeing it glide out of the park in the back of a pickup truck during soccer practice.

Perhaps there is a mystery to be solved here in Mammoth after all. Tom discovered two large metal spikes buried deep into one of the Jeffrey pines in the front yard. He said spikes were once used by tree-huggers to booby trap a tree and potentially inflict injury on loggers. We have no idea why the spikes are there, but it is clear that they have been there for years. What other tales could these trees tell me?

Friday

Red letter day! Of all the questions that I know are haunting you—*Has Jennifer lost any weight? Has she found more soccer socks? Don't these people ever do any work?*—the most riveting must be: *Where do you stand with the expired instant oatmeal?* And yes! Today, Tom ate the last of the horrid expired instant oatmeal.

A schoolmate, Oscar, came over to hang out with Julian this afternoon, and they played chess and pool. Oscar is gangly (all legs and arms), lively, and cheerful.

"Hey, do you use this?" he said, his eyes lighting up when he discovered our gum ball machine.

"Yes!" Tom said, "We use it to, ah… get gum."

Due to a snafu, Luc turns out not to have on-campus housing for the fall quarter at the University of California, Santa Cruz. We spent some time this week looking online for off-campus housing. It was very stressful. There have been times this week when you would not have wanted to be part of our family, like the one where I found myself yelling at the top of my lungs from my writing loft: **"STOP ARGUING!!!!"** In a brighter moment, Tom announced, "Here's a good one. Comcast Internet with triple-speed Xnet!"

"What do I Google?" Luc yelled excitedly from the next room.

After stumbling around without success, we decided Tom and Luc should drive over to Santa Cruz tomorrow morning and see what they manage on the ground. I packed up sweet rolls, sandwiches, granola bars, chips, drinks, fruit, and lots and lots of cookies to fuel them on their drive through Yosemite. We remembered to *not* put the food in the car until morning, and everyone went to bed early.

Saturday

Tom and Luc crawled out of bed at 4:45 a.m., and we packed the car. I watched them drive off before dawn, and when I snuggled back in bed, the covers were still warm. *I dream I hear children laughing, but when I wake up, the house is completely silent.*

There is a deep silence here, very unlike back home. In San Diego, even if the nearby environment is quiet, you can always hear noise if you listen harder. You can hear far-off machinery or the freeway or the ocean. Here, even if something nearby is making a racket, like a chattering squirrel, a cawing crow, or a passing car, behind the noise is an enormous noise vacuum. You feel the silence of the mountains, the rocks, the trees, their solidness and stillness.

Sunday

On the drive home from baseball practice with the sun behind them, the Sierra looked like layered paper cutouts, a large-scale color gradient in shades of gray. The closer slopes were fuzzy with trees in contrast to the smooth and stark ranges further away that rose above the tree line. Julian, Taff, and Will (a tiny eighth-grader who can play the heck out of second base) ignored all of that and were busy comparing local restaurant experiences. Julian recommended Rafters where we went for my mother's eightieth birthday celebration. Will has been to the Red Lantern where he ate a fish eye.

"It was gross," he says. "Crunchy."

"I thought it would be just the opposite," Taff says.

"What, that a fish would eat a human eye?" Julian asks, confused.

"No! That it would be squishy," Taff explains.

"No, look," Will demonstrates. "Feel your eye. That's squishy, right?"

"Yeeeaaaah," Taff says slowly, rubbing his finger around on his eye.

"But like if you take a knife and stick it in a sheep's eye…" Will starts to elaborate.

Not able to take it anymore, I cry out, "Stop! Stop!" and the boys move on to discussing the equity of the recent soccer trades (deemed to be ineffective) and the merits of certain teachers.

"Mrs. Martin, she was so awesome," Will says. "She wouldn't speak Spanish to us even when she was the Spanish teacher."

By some miracle, Tom and Luc found a room in a house in an ideal location and much cheaper than the dorms. My only hesitation was that it was advertised as a "killer house," although the ad also said, "No parties of any kind. We are a STUDIOUS HOUSE-HOLD." They will be home tomorrow.

Monday

With Tom and Luc out of town, it was up to me to get Julian to school on time. *Feeling the pressure of responsibility, I dream that I can't find the appropriate bike gear or his backpack or my house key, and that I wander from room to room in some extremely messy apartment and even lose my way and climb up and down various flights of stairs, unsure if my rooms are on the mezzanine or if I'm even correctly retracing my steps.* In real life, nothing like that happened, and we set out nice and early in the warm sunshine with Mammoth Rock shining down on us like some icon of nature's greatness. I rode back home down the S curves by the community college because they're so fun.

A bear broke into a lodge at June Lake last week and ate a bag of marshmallows, some brown sugar, sausage and cheese, fifteen muffins (I guess he's not worried about gluten), one giant cookie, and one Kit Kat bar. The owner of the lodge described him as a "nuisance bear" and has taken steps to discourage him by putting ammonia-soaked rags on the window and covering the windows so the bear can't see in (apparently bears window-shop). This is the time of year when bears go into hyperphagia, a period of excessive eating and drinking to fatten up for hibernation. I wonder if I can use that excuse.

As subgroups emerge from the "people who live here," I am observing the politics of bumper stickers. Many people here have them on their cars—perhaps as a reflection of their independent frontier spirit—and some cars are plastered with bumper stickers. A common one is the M that looks like an underlined mountain range; that one is a logo for Mammoth Mountain and is selected by snowboarders and Mountain employees. The Mammoth Lakes sticker showing a cartoon drawing of a mountain is for townsfolk or wildlife enthusiasts. The cars of the hard-core people who *really* live here sport the mandatory bumper sticker that says "DON'T FEED OUR BEARS." One wag modified it to read "FEED OUR BEARS DONUTS."

On my afternoon hike, as I descended Old Mammoth Road, I began to hear a banjo, played well and with confidence. After a little investigation, I came across a man, sitting in the sun on the porch of his A-frame cabin, playing and tapping his foot. It was wonderful music and so befitting the setting. Although it did make me think of the *Deliverance*-related bumper sticker I saw at Eagle Lodge: "Paddle faster. I hear banjo music."

Tuesday

I was in the school office this morning for the pledge of allegiance and some announcements. The PA system requires the secretary to stretch two phones cords from opposite sides of the office to the middle of the room where the pledge leader or announcer stands and speaks into both phones at once. We're pretty high tech up here.

A June Lake ski area work crew accidentally started a fire last night, and parts of June have been evacuated. This was big news at school as some of Julian's schoolmates had to leave their homes.

Taff asked one of the boys on the baseball team if his dad was "fighting the fire."

"No," corrected the teammate. "He's managing the fire. *Managing.* Big difference."

I thought there were only two fire stations in Mammoth, but there are three if you count the one staffed by the Forest Service. There are signs throughout the town cautioning us about the danger of fires, such as "One less spark, one less wildfire." Julian and I agreed that the one that says, "Only YOU can prevent forest fires," seems a little overstated.

Wednesday

After taking Julian to school this morning, Tom and I rode over to the historical museum next to Mammoth Creek; it was closed for the winter but is run in the summer by the Southern Mono Historical Society and is housed in an interesting old cabin. We then proceeded down Sherwin Creek Road so I could look at the rocky road that leads all the way down to US 395 near Whitmore, the one that nearly rattled Christine to pieces. After more exploring, we found a dirt road that follows the edge of the woods, up and down the foothills, all the way over to the Snowcreek Condos—a beautiful ride. The road ended at a sandy single track that crossed some exciting bumps and led to a trail that skirted the golf course, marked with menacing "No Trespassing" signs. Following along through flowers and sage bushes, we came up on Old Mammoth Road on the north side of Snowcreek. What a spectacular morning!

Perhaps related to the fire, a helicopter came flying through the valley, startling us with a disturbing and annoying sound we hadn't heard in weeks. It was a rude reminder of how the military aircraft constantly bombarded us with noise from the skies in San Diego. I sure don't miss that.

Unexpectedly, I do miss Petco Park when I see it on television. Julian and I had many happy afternoons there, and the Padres are on a roll. Finally, everyone is singing Alexi Amarista's praises, and he is playing out of his mind, with superb defense and clutch hitting. He looks like he is having the time of his life.

The wind picked up by afternoon, and it was quite blustery down at Whitmore for baseball practice. At the end of the day, the boys were instructed to strap the wheeled batting practice cage to the backstop to secure it against the wind. The thing is huge—sixteen feet by sixteen feet or so—and heavy—it takes six to eight boys to push it in place. I expressed surprise that the wind could move it. "Ohhh, it can really blow down here," one of the dads said to me. "It already got tore up once."

With the smoke in the air from the June Lake fire, the sunset coming home along US 395 was stunning.

September 18–24, 2014
Thursday

Bishop beat Mammoth in football last week 50–0. I'm not making this up. The newspaper stated, "It did not go well for the Mammoth Huskies." Also, the girls' volleyball team did pretty well in a tournament last week until they met Bishop in the finals and lost. *Why is Bishop so good in sports?*

In other news, the drinking beat goes on. A guy showed up for his court date—drunk—and was arrested and taken out of the courtroom in handcuffs. A man was arrested on suspicion of being drunk in public when he was found in his parked car, slumped over the steering wheel with the music blaring and an open container of alcohol next to him. Another man was reported passed out on the Lake Mary bike path after midnight and was arrested for public intoxication.

In the eyebrow-raising story of the week, the police responded to a call about loud music in a mobile home park; while they were there, they observed a man driving too fast through the park. After they stopped him and searched the vehicle, he was arrested on charges related to a switchblade knife they found, as well as driving drunk, driving recklessly, driving without a license, and failing to stop at a stop sign. While all that was going on, *another* drunk guy came over and started yelling obscenities at the police (this is some trailer park), and they arrested him for public intoxication. Either the local police have a high quota, or there's a lot of drinking going on up here.

Tonight was Back to School night, and we took Oscar's mother, Kristen, a dark-haired vivacious beauty, with us. We were surprised to see so few chairs set up in the gymnasium (Kristen counted only one hundred), and many were empty for the principal's welcome and a plea for donations from the PTA. Annie Rinaldi is the principal, with whom I had a long phone conversation back in July. She is half Basque and half Italian, is from New York by way of Los Angeles, has been principal for four years, and told me, "I can't imagine leaving." I was impressed with her enlightened approach to teaching Spanish by hiring native Spanish speakers as teachers.

Her comments this evening were translated into Spanish, paragraph by paragraph, for the Latino parents by an earnest, slightly-flustered woman, whose eyes would open wider and wider as the English words flowed out on and on without giving her a chance at the microphone. This became especially problematic when the PTA president began speaking in breathless, run-on, and unfinished sentences. Everyone else seemed very relaxed.

Just like Back to School night in Del Mar, we scurried from room to room as the teachers ran through their too-long presentations in ten minutes and never left time for questions. None of them had figured out how to distribute the URLs for their web pages, so precious minutes were wasted while parents laboriously copied down curiously long URLs off the computer screen. Some of the teachers seemed rattled by the parents, especially their large presence in the small chairs. "You're kind of big," said the Language Arts teacher.

The PE teacher, Mr. "Let's-Go-Cupcakes" Hensley, pleaded with us to emphasize at home the importance of physical health. He confessed that he is happiest on his bike, and I noticed later a not-insignificant wound on his elbow. The Art thru Writin teacher was sweet and had hung up an autographed poster of Aaron Gwin, a downhill mountain biker who has won the World Cup multiple times.

Some parents looked unusually athletic (one tall blonde looked like she came from Olympus), but most were of average build and very casually dressed. They were mostly quiet, especially the Latino parents. There was a noticeable lack of makeup among the women, and I didn't see a single manicure the entire evening.

The room of the Science teacher was so crammed with materials, posters, signs, and objects that they covered the door and were oozing out into the hallway. Mrs. Vanko, a tiny, animated woman, whose clothes hung scarecrow-fashion, greeted us at the door, clutching a long stick.

"Is that the tardy stick?" Tom asked.

"I might need to point at something," she burbled. Upon learning who we were, she sucked in her breath enthusiastically. "Julian! He's a natural-born scientist," she chirped, holding onto my hand. In front of the group, she explained excitedly that she became a science teacher because her seventh-grade Russian science teacher woke her up to how science is *"everything."*

"I prefer to teach middle school," she said. "You can sometimes still flip the switch in high school, but usually they're too old."

Julian had been talking the night before about how great she is, and I could see why he is thrilled with her. Her classroom is a riotous morass of posters, beakers, chemicals, microscopes, printouts, books, stacks of papers, animal models, and jars and jars of scissors and small tools. The area behind her pull-down screen lies in shadow and conjures up a cave packed with mysterious boxes, stacks of dusty materials, cluttered shelves of weird science stuff, lurking unidentifiable figures, and maybe a hanging skeleton. She is an interesting comparison to my older son's seventh-grade science teacher who sat in the back of the classroom and dozed while the students watched movies.

It turns out that Jill Vanko is married to Jim Vanko, who, as part of the interpretive programs at the ranger station, for years portrayed Red Sotcher, the crusty miner of Sotcher Lake. Jim and Jill were students at Michigan State when he got a job offer with the US Forest Service in Mammoth, a town Jim couldn't even find on the map. An actor in college, Jim came up with the idea of impersonating Sotcher in costume to make history more accessible to children by telling about local events through the eyes of this hardscrabble mountain man. It worked. Using visual effects, the show was a hit, and Jim's theatrical run lasted six years. Although Sotcher was a legendary character, specifics are thin, but he did grow root vegetables along the San Joaquin River in the 1870s. He mined a little, but allegedly had more success as a horse thief, absconding with horses from the west side over the French Trail.

"I have a hunch that there's probably some truth in all of it," Jim said. "He was kind of a shady character."

Friday

The Kamikaze Bike Games are this weekend, and the town is filling up with new cars and LA vanity plates. This event signals the end of summer as the Mammoth Mountain Bike Park will close for the season on Sunday night. Given certain ski executives' delight in getting out on their bikes (ahem—Bill Cockroft), it is no surprise that the ski area became a mountain bike mecca in the 1980s. The bike park now offers hundreds of miles of trails, shuttles, chairs, and gondola lifts to the top where daredevils can try their hand at the Kamikaze trail. A former park manager described the Kamikaze as, "more of an experience. It's kind of like bungee jumping—you want to say you've done it." The mastermind behind many of the trails and events is Cockroft, the amiable longtimer we owe many thanks to for his contribution to the sport.

Riding back from school, I came across Julian's baseball coach and a work crew pulling up flowers along upper Meridian. This seemed rather heartless until an article in the paper shed some light on their activities. A local botanist reported on the invasion of an aggressive aster *from Wyoming* and said it can cross-pollinate with native plants and become a "super weed." It is so dangerous that it is recommended that you put the plant in a sealed plastic bag after you've pulled it out. First bears, now flowers.

The middle school had their first dance tonight, and quite a few of Julian's friends went. We picked up several and drove to the school at 5:30 p.m. One rider tried to remember who he had danced with previously, and another explained that the kids kind of dance as a group except during the "slow ones." Afterwards Julian said he had a pretty good time. He said he had danced with a sixth-grader and an eighth-grader.

"Did they ask you?" I asked.

"Nah-oh," he said, making a face as though I were an idiot.

"No one would ask him," Luc said, mocking.

"**Shut up**, Luc. You're not man enough to ask a girl to dance," Julian said, and that was the end of that.

Saturday

Rumors have floated that Julian's soccer coach, Alex, "quit" the team in protest over the team's poor performance. But the stories have been so muddled that, as one player's dad put it, "I don't know what I've heard." If the resignation was intended to fire up the troops, it failed, as the boys went down 0–3 to Bishop. Kristen's son is also on the team, and she just keeps saying she's never seen a soccer season like this. Besides the apathy and lack of team spirit, the team looked *tired.* Maybe it's the altitude.

Tom and Luc rode their bikes down to Whitmore from Mammoth on the body-rattling, teeth-chattering gravel Sherwin Creek Road to watch the game. Tom described it as a long sweeping downhill ride. Luc described it differently. I'll spare you the obscenities.

Sunday

Julian's prize from the Del Mar summer reading program arrived! It's a twenty-dollar gift certificate from Target. The Internet says the nearest Target is 184 miles away. Instead, we went to Kmart and Smart & Final in Bishop after the baseball game, along with the other Mammoth parents.

The baseball coach had organized a mini-tournament this weekend with teams from Mammoth Lakes, Bishop, Dayton, and Tehachapi. Those Tehachapi parents drove three hours to participate, and I have no idea how far Dayton is. Although there were no official scores, Bishop beat up the high school team, but Julian's team prevailed against Bishop's fourteen and under. The boys played better, and the catcher and Julian at third executed a great play to pick a guy off. It was perfect—except when the umpire called him safe.

All this driving reminded me that a baseball mom had warned me about all the "schlepping" Mammoth Lakes parents do. Last year, the baseball team participated in a tournament three hours away, and they drove there *twice.* "Welcome to Mammoth," she said dourly.

Monday

The days are falling into a routine, a cycle of baseball and soccer practice, rides to school, reading and writing, minimal cleaning or working, and glorious daily hikes among the pines under magnificent blue skies. Three days a week, Julian and Oscar ride their bikes from school down the sidewalk to the tunnel that takes them under Main Street and onto the bike path down to Shady Rest for soccer practice. The ride is car free except for the section on Sierra Star Parkway which—at worst—is right next to the hospital. At the park, they do homework or wrestle while waiting for the other kids to show up. I usually go down, sit in the sun, read, and wonder if it will really ever snow.

Tuesday

The normal middle school schedule was cancelled today so that the students could participate in a school-wide run on the Mammoth Rock Trail. They were bused to the lower trailhead and ran *up* the 2.6 miles. I hoped to catch some of the fun, but by the time I hiked down the Panorama Dome Trail, they had already been picked up and taken to Shady Rest for games. It was a fantastic hike through deep woods, then onto a sandy trail that skirts Mammoth Rock, and down onto the meadow trail that connects to Sherwin Creek Road. The flora and fauna appeared to have survived the kids' passage as all was calm, with only the sounds of the breeze and birds, although one black squirrel did scream at me quite hysterically and then ran off. In my mind's eye, I imagined the six hundred running feet, chatter, laughter, rough housing, excitement, and whispers that make up the social politics of middle school. In their wake, I found two water bottles, a Pepsi can, wrappers from a granola bar and a Jolly Rancher, a name tag, and a Band-Aid.

I came across a very elegant gray bird with velvet black wings striped in white. It looked as though he was headed off to a ball at the Met. My list of Mammoth Lakes birds and the Internet led me to determine that it was a Clark's nutcracker, although my bird's wings seemed bigger and blacker.

Report from Boston: My four-year-old niece has set up her bedside table with an alarm clock, a flashlight, and a water gun. My brother-in-law said it reminded him of Houston. Maybe they should move to Mammoth and calm down.

Wednesday

After dropping Julian at school and another trip to the transfer station, Tom and I stopped by the grocery store, so that he could transport a hundred pounds of food home in the trailer. We made a bit of a scene in Vons with our helmets and bike gear. The cashier studied the blinky light attached to Tom's helmet and said to me sotto voce, "Is he solar powered?"

As the driver of the carpool back from Whitmore tonight, I was honored to be transporting two of the fastest runners from the Mammoth Rock Run—Oscar came in third, and tiny Will came in first place with a time of 22:25 that broke the school record that *he* set last year! I tried to engage the boys about the news that Mammoth Mountain Ski Area has bought Big Bear and Snow Summit for $38 million, even though their CEO openly acknowledged that "this isn't a very good time to be buying a ski resort." They were not very interested in that and not at all in the last streaming rays of sunlight coming over the Sierra in a dazzling display.

A lens cloud perched
over the Sierra peak
murmurs, just you wait

IN WHICH WE CONFRONT WHAT WE HAVE DONE

*She's a great friend, but if you are a bitch to her,
she'll be a bitch to you. So watch out.*

~ DEFINITION OF *SIERRA* FROM THE URBAN DICTIONARY

September 25–28, 2014

Thursday

WHEE! WHILE I was making Julian's breakfast this morning, a powerful gust of wind hit the house. Tom warned us last night that things were about to change, or as people up here say, "we're going to get some weather." Tom and I put on jackets, tights, and headbands for our daily ride; Julian still wore his customary T-shirt, long-sleeved flannel shirt, and shorts.

"Mom's going to have to put rocks in her pocket when she goes hiking today," Tom told Julian. It *was* intense up on Lake Mary Road.

8:30 p.m.

Oh, no! It's happened. We've just had an earthquake. During my first trip to Mammoth as Tom's here-to-be-evaluated girlfriend, an earthquake shook the house, which scared me, and Tom's parents laughed and laughed. I am not an irrational person. I am afraid of earthquakes because things can fall down and then you won't have anyplace to sleep that night. I am also afraid of snakes because they can bite you from hidden places and you will have to go to the hospital. I am also afraid of heights because if you fall from them you will die. I am not afraid of spiders, flying, close quarters, or blood because those fears are dumb.

The 3.9 earthquake gave my writing loft a good hard shake, but only one. I learned that this quake was part of a "swarm," a series of earthquakes that began this morning, of which six were over 3.0. It was the biggest swarm in a decade and a reminder that we are living near young volcanoes. The swarm came from the Long Valley Caldera (remember the caldera?) and was the result of the release of gases through magma—not the movement of magma. The geologists are all excited and think this is very interesting. Me, I'm reconsidering this whole undertaking. Maybe we can get our Del Mar house back.

Friday

We have a cloud! This morning it looked as though someone stuck a shock of white hair on top of Mammoth Mountain. Tom busied himself researching weather forecasts for the house, Whitmore field, and Tioga Pass to plan our weekend. The bottom line was that it might rain. Or snow. Or neither.

We rode through the woods east of Shady Rest this morning on a mountain bike trail that is converted to a cross-country ski trail in the winter. The woods are lovely, and it was fun dodging pine cones. We came across one of the controversial geothermal plant wells with a positively enormous water pipe running out toward US 395.

Saturday

Suddenly, we are freezing. The temperature dropped to an overnight low in the thirties, and it snowed lightly this morning for about an hour. There is a dusting of snow on the White Mountains. Instead of worrying about heat stroke at the soccer game, we were trying to think up a way to serve hot drinks. The boys wore sweatshirts and long pants under their uniforms, and the parents told stories about clearing snow from the field last year so the boys could play. Oscar told us how much it hurts to fall in the snow, and, of course, you fall more often when you're playing in snow.

Consistent with how soccer rolls in Mammoth, we learned two days ago that we were snack family this week. Here's how we found out: Tom went over to introduce himself to Coach Alex, saying, "Hi. I just wanted to say 'hi.' I'm Tom, Julian's dad?"

Alex shook his hand and said, "Nice to meet you. Would you be the snack family on Saturday?"

Tom made chocolate chip cookies, and, unlike Del Mar where the boys politely declined homemade goods, here the soccer participants snarfed them down, even the center ref. Tom didn't get a single one, a travesty from which he may never recover.

Saturday

It has dawned on us that living on the east side of the Sierra while one's son is attending college in Santa Cruz might pose some challenges when Tioga Pass closes. We could be in for some long drives in the winter. For now, Tom will drive Luc up to Yosemite tomorrow morning through the pass; then, for a total of forty-four dollars, Luc will catch a series of trains and buses to Santa Cruz to start the fall semester.

Sunday

Ah. Well. The pass did close last night. This interfered with our plans considerably—which is a polite way of saying they got totally f***ed-up. After panicking, Tom set his alarm to go off every half hour during the night to check the closure status. And the pass suddenly reopened at 9:00 a.m. with no restrictions—no chains, no nothing. *How could that be?* With no time to worry about that, we threw Tom and Luc in the car and hurled food and luggage after them, and they left at 9:11 a.m. Catching the 10:30 a.m. bus from Yosemite was hopeless, but they had a fighting chance (so they said) of making the train from Merced at 1:08 p.m. I checked the timing on MapQuest—it reported that the drive would take three hours and fifty-six minutes. That would get them there with one minute to spare.

I don't know what that drive was like, and I don't really want to; I heard some reports of aggressive passing and squealing tires—quickly denied—so who can say. They allegedly made good time through the pass and were starting to relax slightly once they reached SR 140 until they came upon a crew using cables to pull a truck that had gone off the edge of the cliff back up onto the highway. This halted traffic in both directions for twenty minutes. Agitated, Tom got out and chatted with the local in front of him who explained that Tioga Pass closes immediately when there is a threat of ice. That's why there were no chain restrictions when it reopened.

When the road opened, they were again in a minute-by-minute race to get to the train in Merced. Not wanting to risk being stopped by the CHP, they pushed the edge of every speed limit and flew down the long straightaway into Merced, glancing from the road to the GPS to the speedometer back to the road, until the train station was in sight. Luc had called Amtrak for an update on the train's departure time; it was late—it would leave at 1:11 p.m., a blessing of three minutes. Waiting for an old lady who was sl-ow-ly sl-ow-ly making a right turn, they panicked when the crossing bar up the street came down—until they realized the train station was on their side of the bar. They hurtled into the parking lot, and Luc sprang from the car with his luggage and dashed toward the train. Most passengers had already loaded, but the train's doors were miraculously still open.

"Did Dad tell you about getting to the train?" Luc asked me later by telephone.

"Yeah, he said you made it with only a couple minutes to spare," I said.

"Um. Yeah. I'd say about *one* minute," Luc said.

That's taking my rule to never break stride while traveling a bit too far.

After he saw Luc safely onto the train, parked, and caught his breath, Tom sat down on a bench at the station to call me: he said his plan was to carefully buy gas, drive slowly and cautiously up the pass, and maybe have a little picnic lunch in Yosemite before he came out on our side of the mountains. It was not to be.

Now, one would think that Julian and I would have considered the consequences when we looked up from our game of Battleship that afternoon and saw that it was, in fact, raining. Uh, no. It never occurred to us that rain could spell dire events on the pass. Fortunately, Tom is smarter than we are; it began raining as he passed the site of the truck's departure and reemergence sans driver, so he cancelled his lunch plans and began to hasten up the mountain. The race was back on! So while Julian and I mindlessly continued our games and made ourselves a snack, Tom was again pushing the speed limits and testing the Toyota's traction to get through the pass twice in one piece and in one day.

In retrospect, there are things that we could have done differently—that could have saved us some stress—but sometimes events fall one after another, unpredictable and surprising, while we, like shells in the tide, are rocked first one way and then another and can only grapple with each moment and try to stay afloat and hope that in the end at least we'll get a good story out of it. Tom made it home safe and sound, Luc transitioned from Merced to Stockton to San Jose and on to Santa Cruz without incident, and we spent considerable time that evening thanking our lucky stars and trying not to think about what-ifs.

HOW DO I GET TO SANTA CRUZ FROM HERE?

"It's tough here. The dating sites are always trying to hook you up with guys in Fresno because it looks as though you're geographically close on the map."

~ OVERHEARD AT A LOCAL RECEPTION

THE ONE HUNDRED sixty miles of the ridge of the Sierra Nevada from Yosemite to Sequoia National Park is the longest expanse of wilderness in the continental United States that remains uncut by any road. It is bound in the north by Tioga Pass (SR 120) and in the south by Walker Pass (SR 178), both of which close in the winter, compelling those who need to cross the mountains to travel even further north or south. The pristine backbone of the mountain range resembles a gigantic slumbering armored ankylosaurus whose immensity and fierce snores made even the most intrepid highway builders pause. The entire Sierra Nevada is a seventy-mile-wide, four-hundred-mile-long block that reaches from Mount Lassen to the Tehachapi Mountains. Its massive granite bulk includes Mount Whitney, the highest peak in the continental United States, at 14,500 feet. The Sierra Nevada represents the single most imposing geological barrier in the country. Tell me about it. A student at the University of California, Santa Cruz, during our time in Mammoth Lakes, my older son experienced a new adventure in crossing the bulwark during every school break.

The dead of winter was the "easiest" time because Luc could take the daily flight from San Francisco to Mammoth Lakes. He just had to take the bus from campus to downtown Santa Cruz, catch the Route 17 bus to San Jose, and take the Caltrain to Millbrae station where he could pick up the BART to the airport. That route left him only at risk of flight cancellations because of bad weather, usually in Mammoth—which did occur regularly. Occasionally when the airlines had overbooked the flight, he lucked out and sold his seat back to them; more often his traveling experience was one of delays and discomfort. To catch the flight out of SFO, he either had to get up at 3:00 a.m. and trust that he would make all his connections or go up the night before and spend the night at the airport. Once he arrived at SFO to discover the flight was cancelled, and the airline couldn't get him on a flight for two days. Facing the prospect of a lengthy stay at the airport or the long return to Santa Cruz, he flew to San Diego to catch a ride up to Mammoth with a friend.

Crossing in non-winter months was even harder as there were no flights from Northern California. Once he used the bus-bus-train option to get to Santa Clarita where he drove up with his uncle who was coming for Thanksgiving. Several times, we drove over Tioga Pass in the minivan to retrieve him along with his belongings, but the twelve-hour round trip—even longer when SR 17 into Santa Cruz was jammed—was not a pleasant drive. I became increasingly appreciative of why most of our visitors came from Southern California and not the Bay Area, since they can make the relatively easy drive up Owens Valley instead of across the ankylosaurus.

Echo Summit and I-80 over Donner Summit are the two nearest passes to Mammoth Lakes that are reliably kept open all winter, but those routes add hours to our journey compared to the Tioga route. Echo Summit is traversed by today's US 50, which travels from Sacramento to the Nevada state line. Developed from the Lake Tahoe Wagon Road, it was designated California's first official state highway. Its storied history includes its use during the gold rush by the '49ers and later by travelers coming to and from the Comstock Lode. The major road through the Sierra in the 1860s, it was the route chosen by the Pony Express in their first year of operation.

The maiden eastbound run of the Pony Express took place April 4, 1860, and was nearly disrupted by snow in the Sierra. Heavy snow obscured the wagon trail, and the rider, Warren Upson, was obliged to dismount and lead his horse to find his way. It took him an entire day to cover the eighty-five miles to Carson City, but, despite the terrible snow conditions, the mail had gotten through! There Upson waited for the first westbound Express. Then the poor boy had the opposite problem—the weather had cleared, and wagons and pack trains clogged the route, forcing the rider and his horse to plunge into deep snow on the side of the road to pass.

The Pony Express riders, in general, had a tough time, although the job was candidly advertised. The wanted poster read, "Young, skinny, wiry fellows not over eighteen. Must be expert riders, willing to risk death daily. Orphans preferred." Upson, however, was no orphan; he was the son of the editor of the *Sacramento Union*. The Express had no shortage of candidates; the exciting job appealed to young hotheads, and the pay was good at one hundred dollars a month. "Buffalo Bill" Cody himself signed on at the age of fourteen.

Worse than snow, Indian attacks disrupted the mail services during the month of May, causing the Express to briefly suspend operations after several employees were killed and their horses stolen. Eighteen months later, the invention of the telegraph and the American Civil War dealt a death blow to the celebrated Pony Express, whose riders and horses have so captured our imagination.

Carson Pass is closer to Mammoth Lakes than Echo Summit and is often open in the winter, but the journey over it on SR 88 adds a couple hours to the trip. It also was a major thoroughfare for the gold rush traffic and became a toll road in 1860s. Carson Pass is named for "Kit" Carson who, depending on your viewpoint, was either a bloodthirsty Indian killer or a heroic mountain guide who opened up the West for settlement. In the winter of 1844, Carson was traveling with US army officer John C. Frémont as part of his second overland expedition to map parts of the West. Frémont's group attempted to cross the Sierra from Nevada and became blocked by snow. They resorted to eating their stock until Carson found a way through the pass. Their struggle foreshadowed the dangerous traps that lay in wait for others who would attempt to cross the Sierra in winter.

Ebbetts Pass and Sonora Pass are even closer to Mammoth Lakes than Carson Pass, but they are only open five months of the year. Ebbetts Pass was the site of the first white-man Sierra crossing in 1827 when explorer Jedediah Smith and his men scrambled over the snow-covered barrier from their camp along the Stanislaus River to Topaz Lake. Now traversed by SR 4, a designated scenic highway, Ebbetts is one of the least-traveled passes because of its extreme hairpin turns and lack of a center line.

Sonora Pass was used by immigrants in the 1840s and was developed as a commercial road once silver was discovered on the east side. The second-highest pass, it reaches 9,624 feet and is extremely steep; its grade exceeds 8 percent most of the way and goes up to 26 percent in places. If you don't die of fright, it is extraordinarily lovely with spectacular views. As SR 108, it crosses the Pacific Crest Trail, the twenty-six-hundred-fifty-mile-long trail that extends from Canada to Mexico, so you can hop out, hike a short distance, and dream of being in the tattered shoes of those who go the distance.

The highest pass road, Tioga Pass Road, is nearest to Mammoth Lakes, but it closes at the drop of a hat, or at the drop of the thermometer, because its normal treachery becomes multifold when the road turns icy. It closes permanently in late fall and doesn't reopen until all threat of snow is gone in early summer. It isn't just snow that keeps the road closed. For weeks in the spring, roped-in scalers crawl over the outcroppings above the roadway to knock down and collect loose rocks before the highway can open.

The route followed by the Tioga Road was developed from the Great Sierra Wagon Road, an old pack and wagon road used since 1849 by prospectors and miners, and eventually by nature lovers, to access Yosemite Valley. By 1910, state engineers had constructed a road from Lee Vining on the east side up to the pass with a maximum grade of 7 percent, quite an engineering feat at the time. In 1915, Stephen Mather, the future first director of the National Park Service, became determined to develop the road. He raised sufficient funds to purchase the road from private interests and donated the hairy twenty-one-mile-long midsection to Yosemite National Park. It opened immediately to cars, but the adventurous route was described as a "roller coaster, only rougher," and confident driving skills were recommended.

As it became more heavily used in the 1920s, the federal highway engineers installed culverts and bridges. Nevertheless, in his book *The Kid from Mono Mills*, Augie Hess recalls that it took a full day to get from Lee Vining to Yosemite Valley: cars overheated and drivers had to wait their turn on the one-way road down into the valley. During odd hours the cars would go down, and during even hours the cars would come up the steep road with its multiple switchbacks.

The National Park Service continued to push for more road improvements, supported by the Sierra Club and Bureau of Public Roads, who wanted to reroute and widen the road. Road construction expert Walter L. Huber was consulted, and he advised that a "park road" be constructed. Such a road would hold two, ten-foot-wide lanes and a slightly wider-than-normal shoulder of four feet because, Huber said, "once a motorist is over the edge, he is often in trouble"—a contender for the understatement of the decade.

The proposal caused a major rift inside the Sierra Club. Some powerful members, including photographer Ansel Adams, were horrified by the proposed route that would relocate the road up to Tenaya Lake and even require dynamiting some of the granite domes at the heart of the high country. "Tenaya Lake is infinitely more important than the Park Service," groused Adams. Nevertheless, the state pushed ahead, and the road was built and paved at a cost of $7 million. At its dedication in 1961, the National Park Service director stated defensively, "I make no apologies for the Tioga Road."

After the section through Lee Vining Canyon was rebuilt in the late 1960s, the Tioga Road, in its final configuration, covers 6,000 feet of elevation change across its sixty miles and as SR 120 represents one of the most significant highway building endeavors in the country. It rises to an astonishing 9,945 feet. I could say that the views from the road are spectacular, but that would imply that I have looked out at them. I've attempted to do as little of that as possible by keeping my eyes fixed on the road above my white-knuckle grip on the steering wheel.

As predicted by opponents, it is a difficult road full of hairpin turns and switchbacks, and high speeds have led to fatalities; drownings, falls, and heart attacks in Yosemite, however, far outnumber the car-related deaths on Tioga Pass. The biggest threat is the overheating of people's tempers when obliged to slow down on a mountain road.

In comparison, the high-speed interstate through Donner Summit on I-80 looks like a model of safety, decreasing from six lanes to four only over the crest. It roars east out of Sacramento, begins to climb from the Central Valley floor at 1,400 feet and rises to "only" 7,239 feet at Donner Summit before it descends into Truckee. It closely follows the Central Pacific Railroad route, the western section of the first transcontinental railroad. The interstate carries an average of forty- to fifty-thousand cars and trucks over the pass on a typical day, but the circulation can double on holidays as travelers head out for a weekend of skiing, boating, biking, or gambling.

Nevertheless, I-80 is notorious for winter-related accidents and fatalities as its heavy traffic tangles with the annual thirty-six feet of snow that falls on Donner Summit. The National Geographic Channel ran a documentary series about the men and women who work to keep the road open, especially the tow-truck drivers, describing the danger and carnage they face. Accompanied by a driving rock music score, the episodes were replete with stunning car crashes, overturned big rigs, near misses, body bags, blowing snow, and black ice. The series was appropriately called *Hell on the Highway.*

In an attempt to maintain order, the California Department of Transportation operates a series of stations distributed along the seventy-six miles from Auburn to the Nevada state line. Caltrans employees avail themselves of nearly one hundred fifty heavy duty vehicles in their snow- and ice- fighting arsenal: plows, snowblowers, sanders, rotary ice-breakers, graders, loaders, fuel trucks, and—you guessed it—tow trucks. They also use extremely heavy trucks that are capable of pushing a stopped big rig forward to regain its traction and keep traffic flowing. A major machine shop operates year-round to keep all this equipment in order and to design new customized vehicles.

The pressure of commercial traffic poses a special challenge as the interstate serves as the major thoroughfare for goods traveling from Northern California ports to the rest of the country; over four million dollars' worth of goods flow over Donner Summit *every hour.* Caltrans attempts to keep the big trucks and cars from tangling with each other when dangerous conditions exist. Trucks may be turned back or ordered off the road to park and wait for better weather although fuel, livestock, and mail are allowed to go through if the road remains open to cars. Even today, mail is still a priority.

When road conditions are bad or accidents have occurred, the California Department of Transportation occasionally works in concert with CHP to limit the flow of traffic by reducing three lanes of eastbound traffic to two and then down to one at higher elevations. When chain controls are in effect, vehicles are directed into special parking areas to install chains or have them installed. Those without chains are turned back. As you can imagine, all this equipment and manpower cost money. Keeping I-80 open year-round costs Californians an average of $6 million annually, 27 percent of the state's entire annual snow clearance expenses.

In the olden days, before snow removal budgets and chain controls, crossing through Donner Pass was only safe in summer months, a lesson learned the hard way by a band of immigrants in the winter of 1846–47. Known as the Donner Party after it elected George Donner as its captain, the large group of families, wagons, and livestock was on its way to California from the Midwest. They became trapped by snow, and nearly half of the group's eighty-seven members died, victims of hypothermia, starvation, and other cruelties. Donner Pass was named for their sensational tragedy and serves as a reminder of the kind of catastrophe that the Sierra Nevada can blindly wreak.

Illustration – Minaret Vista US Forest Service Station

FINISH THE HIGHWAY!

As I recall, her name is "Lady," as indeed
she is. Please give her my regards.

~ LETTER FROM GOVERNOR RONALD REAGAN

WE, THE DONNER Party, and Kit Carson weren't the only ones inconvenienced by the mountain range. Back in the 1950s, residents on the west side of the Sierra began to advocate for a new highway that would traverse the range, with Mammoth Lakes at the east end and an outlet near Fresno on the west side. Fresno's main industry was agriculture whose produce required shipment several hundred miles to the north or south to reach markets in the rest of the country. Developers and other business people could see how they would benefit from the thoroughfare, and the Fresno Chamber of Commerce pressured politicians to find funds to build a new highway. Folks on the east side of the Sierra, some with business interests in keeping out more roads, were appalled by the proposal. They felt that the ten existing highways that already crossed the range were enough. The ensuing fight over the road, recounted in Jack Fisher's excellent book, *Stopping the Road*, would pit the Westside against the Eastside and spread from our little region to Sacramento, and finally to the nation's capital, where some unlikely but powerful forces would join the fray.

In 1931, the secretary of agriculture moved the boundaries of two adjacent wilderness areas in order to open up a five-mile gap for an eventual highway south of Yosemite. Over the next decades, supporters of a new road would use various arguments to paint the corridor as an untapped opportunity, just begging to be filled in. With WWII on the horizon, they pointed out that a military route across the Sierra would facilitate the transport of weapons. In 1941, the *Fresno Bee* reported pending legislation for construction of a highway over Mammoth Pass. Apparently the military showed more winter smarts than the legislators and recognized that the transport of heavy military equipment would be unthinkable across a mountain highway, especially one with a summit at 9,300 feet that would be under constant threat of closure. No steps were taken to proceed with local road building during the war. Then, a 1946 *Fresno Bee* headline declared, "Road still needed." This time, the paper suggested that a highway would facilitate access to natural resources, such as iron, silver, and tungsten, though there was little evidence of significant deposits of any of those elements. At the beginning of the Cold War, it was argued that a nearby trans-Sierra crossing was necessary so residents on the west side could escape from a nuclear attack. Most of those claims weren't taken very seriously, but starting in the late 1950s, the drive to build another year-round trans-Sierra highway began to gain momentum.

The interstate highway system grew out of the 1956 Federal-Aid Highway Act that provided 90 percent of construction costs to states who could pony up the first 10 percent. The resulting road construction frenzy produced I-10 and I-40 to the south and I-80 and I-90 to the north, stretching across the country from coast to coast. I-70, however, which crosses the middle of the country, heads west from Baltimore and ends abruptly south of Salt Lake City. The resulting blank space on the map, with no east-west interstate highways, bothered completists, and they took up the cry to "finish" I-70 and use a route near Mammoth Lakes to cross the Sierra.

The *Fresno Bee* ran numerous pro-road editorials, although the writers were somewhat clueless about the possible route. They suggested it should come through Mammoth Pass along a pack trail known as the Old French Trail. The passageway had a long history as a trade route when supplies were brought during the late 1800s from the Fresno Flats to Mammoth City, a booming mining community. That was before it all went bust when it was discovered that there was no gold in these here hills. The proposal was getting traction until highway construction engineers pointed out, unhelpfully, that such a route was geographically infeasible because of the steep terrain and that it didn't even run through the highway corridor created in 1931. Politicians also recognized that the improvement of an existing thoroughfare would be easier to push through the legislature than the development of a brand new road on the back of an old trading route.

Thrashing around for an alternative, highway advocates began to eye FH 100, a narrow track used since the 1920s to pierce the wilderness for fire control and logging. Supporters claimed that a mere fourteen miles of hiking trails would need to be converted to pavement to connect with the forest road's terminus at Reds Meadow pack station. From there, the road ascends a treacherous, winding 2,000 feet, up to Minaret Summit at an elevation of 9,265 feet. Built in the 1930s, it is a harrowing drive even today, mostly one lane with pullouts and extreme drop offs.

Although business people on the east side of the Sierra would also stand to benefit from a major thoroughfare, Mammoth Lakes residents, many of whom were nature lovers, generally opposed the proposed road. Even the Mammoth Lakes Chamber of Commerce consistently stated their opposition to the road. More predictably, also against the highway were packers whose stations were sure to suffer if nature enthusiasts could visit the backcountry by car, rather than by mule or horse.

Local residents were acutely aware of how roads could change the character and prospects of a town. After the town had established itself in a meadow along Mammoth Creek, the state built a new highway, SR 203, which ran from US 395 through undeveloped land up to the lakes basin, completely bypassing the existing town. In short order, shrewd business owners picked up and moved from the meadow over to the new highway. Those left behind saw their businesses suffer. The town had learned what can happen when roads are built.

Highway opponents began to organize a grassroots counter effort and formed the Mono County Resources Committee to fight back. Business people joined in, such as Bob and Peggy Schotz who owned the Woods Lodge on Lake George; Edelweiss Lodge owner, Chip Van Nattan; Doug Kittredge of Kittredge Sports; developer Tom Dempsey; and Lou and Marye Roeser who ran the Mammoth Pack Station. Genny Smith (then Schumacher), a Reed College graduate and local naturalist, served as liaison and general fact-checker for the committee, organizing letter-writing efforts and documenting various initiatives. The informal group had a loose connection to renowned photographer and nature lover Ansel Adams through the Sierra Club.

Although they didn't know it yet, the Mono County Resources Committee was joined in opposition to the highway by influential Norman "Ike" Livermore, owner of the Mount Whitney Pack Train and largest wilderness outfitter in the Sierra Nevada. A road initiative back in the 1930s had set him on red hot alert for any proposals that would not only impact his packer business but also desecrate the wilderness he had come to love while working summers as a student packer.

Livermore was educated at Harvard and Stanford where he received an MBA, for which he wrote his thesis on the wilderness packing business. Livermore moved with his family to the Sierra in 1946 when he went to work for the Pacific Lumber Company. That apparently didn't preclude him from a prominent role in the Sierra Club where he rose to serve on the board of directors. The Sierra Club had a history of making ambivalent statements about wilderness roads, and Livermore worked to strengthen their anti-road position. He and the executive director, David Brower, released a policy statement that declared "there is no justification for dividing a priceless wilderness; therefore, no new road building across the Sierra."

Brower spoke to the Fresno and Madera County Boards of Supervisors in 1956 and said, "The public interest is best served if... the wilderness zone remain[s] unspoiled." The supervisors would not have agreed on a good day, but as Congress had just passed the interstate highway bill, they were lit with the idea that millions of dollars would soon be headed their way to fund road building. In addition, the Cold War was fueling fears, and one of the Madera supervisors maintained that a new crossing would "give the people in San Joaquin Valley their rightful highway outlet to the east should coastal cities become targets of nuclear attack." The notion of evacuating millions of people through a steep winding forest road is dubious, but it was not a time for excessive rational thought. The US Bureau of Public Roads announced that a preliminary survey of a trans-Sierra highway by way of Mammoth Lakes would be undertaken.

When the report came out two years later, the Mono County Resources Committee was poised to react. The report, written by regional engineer Sheridan Farin, claimed that a new thoroughfare would be "feasible" as a forest highway but that its exact location was yet to be determined. He surely did not anticipate that such a tepid conclusion would provoke the fiery response he received from the Mammoth crowd. Genny Smith burst into action and organized a letter-writing campaign. Farin was bombarded with letters that questioned how a road with an unknown location could be considered feasible. He received so many requests for copies of the report that mailing that one document exceeded his entire annual postage budget. The *Fresno Bee* welcomed the report more enthusiastically and reported that the "Mammoth Pass" highway was now backed by a federal agency.

In 1960, legislation was proposed to include the Mammoth Pass Road in the forest highway system, and a series of public hearings were scheduled over the objections of the Sierra Club, the Wilderness Society, and the Nature Conservancy. The hearing in Fresno was especially pro-highway. One geographically challenged advocate spoke of citizens having an "unalienable right to fresh lettuce," seemingly unaware that most of her salad makings would come from the Central Valley.

This apparent progress of the proposal alarmed Raymond J. Sherwin, a judge who lived near Sacramento with deep roots in the Eastern Sierra. He owned a cabin in Mammoth Lakes, and his great-grandfather had built the first road from Bishop to Mammoth and operated it as a toll road. In 1916, the state took over that section and made it the first portion of the California state highway system built east of the Sierra. In the 1930s, it literally paved the way for development of Mammoth Mountain because it significantly shortened the travel time for visitors from the south. Today, this section is still known as the Sherwin Grade.

The judge had strong connections in Sacramento and could follow events related to the highway initiative. He was also intensely opposed and issued a newsletter in 1963, debunking the need for such a crossing. He stated that its importance for national defense had been refuted, that it was not needed for timber harvest, that there were no large iron ore or tungsten deposits, and that large trucks carrying produce would make better time by going over Donner Summit. Sherwin understood that the highway still lacked a funding source, but he wanted to dispose of the arguments in favor of it before the fight for money was undertaken. In keeping with the terminology of the time, his newsletter was titled the *Mammoth Pass Road Newsletter*, though he certainly knew that the highway would not go over Mammoth Pass. He often said that nobody on the west side really understood the geography of the area. Unfortunately for his cause, he was soon to encounter one who did.

The highway advocates gained a powerful ally in Bernie Sisk, US representative from California's 16th congressional district, a Democrat who upended his district's longstanding Republican affiliation. He was elected in 1955 and would serve twelve terms. By 1964, he was publicly calling for accelerated funding of the preliminary studies for the trans-Sierra highway, which he was careful to call the "Minaret Summit Road," not the "Mammoth Pass Road." He announced the support of the Federal Bureau of Roads, the US Forest Service, the National Park Service, and the state, although he privately acknowledged funding would be problematic. One naysayer was quoted in the press as saying that it would take forty years to secure money for the highway. Sisk determined that his first goal would be to get it designated as a state highway. Maintenance costs, including snow removal, for roads built with federal funds remained the obligation of the local authorities, and Sisk wisely recognized that those costs would be impossible for his small communities to bear.

In 1966, the California Division of Highways produced a report that analyzed the cost and benefit of the proposed thoroughfare. The evaluation was thorough and its conclusions devastating for highway advocates. The trans-Sierra route via Minaret Summit, from I-5 to the Nevada state line, would rise from an elevation of 500 feet to 9,260 feet and descend down to 5,000 feet. Cost of construction was estimated at $100 million, annual maintenance at $5.2 million, and annual snow clearance at an additional $1.3 million, which represented almost 20 percent of the state's entire budget for snow removal at that time. The report concluded that "no portion of this proposed route should be added to the state highway system."

Highway supporters panicked. A Fresno County spokesman vowed to get the highway built "no matter the opposition," and Sisk announced that he would travel to Sacramento to "plead for the future welfare of the people of California." The *Fresno Bee* stated that the report would be reviewed in more detail while the Bridgeport newspaper crowed, "Minaret Highway Doomed."

Critics of the report argued the division had gone too far in considering a freeway built to interstate standards and all that was desired was a highway built to forest highway standards. The division was directed to revise its report to evaluate a two-lane forty-miles-per-hour road. A few months later, the highway division released its revised, though essentially unchanged, report. Such a highway did not pass economic feasibility standards because of its cost and low traffic.

Highway supporters regrouped and introduced new legislation to make FH 100 a state responsibility. The bill did not reference the highway division's report and estimates. Instead, it included an estimate of construction costs of $20 million (a number Sisk made up) and ignored snow removal costs. It also made the eyebrow-raising claim that thirty-two of the seventy-eight miles were already in place as a paved road; in reality whatever sections of FH 100 had been paved were only single lane with a few pullouts—and a far cry from a forest highway. Sisk and crew held a press conference and announced, "It is not a matter of whether the road will be built but rather when and what type." A public hearing was set by the transportation committee for April 1967.

The Mammoth Lakes gang moved smoothly into action again and reorganized themselves under the name The John Muir Trail Association as recommended by Judge Sherwin, now serving as an officer. Genny Smith maintained her role as scribe and publicist, releasing notices of factual information and countering arguments made by the highway advocates. The association also benefited from the financial support of developer Tom Dempsey.

Meanwhile, Ike Livermore had been appointed resources secretary under Governor Ronald Reagan, and he continued to criticize the proposed highway. He spoke to the Sierra Club and declared that the crossing "would cut across the John Muir Trail, the very heart and soul of wilderness... I say stop that road." His opposition made the front page of the *San Francisco Examiner*. Genny Smith was in attendance at that speech, giving her the opportunity to meet Livermore, which represented the beginning of a strong partnership in the fight against the highway.

Prior to the hearing, the transportation committee began to receive letters opposing the legislation. Ike Livermore wrote individually to each member. A spokesperson for the Pacific Intermountain Express wrote to explain that because of the crossing's elevation and grade, independent of weather conditions, the "motor carrier industry would not be able to use such a highway." He had just demolished one of the arguments made by highway advocates.

What the Eastern Sierra snow connoisseurs had recognized immediately was the challenge of keeping a 9,265-foot-high pass open year-round. The Mammoth Lakes contingent was well aware of how expensive it would be and intended to emphasize that point at the public hearing. The group felt there was a lack of appreciation for how much more snow there would be at 9,265 feet than on I-80, the closest trans-Sierra highway that was kept open year-round and topped out at 7,239 feet. The president of the Mammoth Lakes Chamber of Commerce remembered one notable meeting in town in which a Fresno representative dared to lecture the group about snow removal before he was interrupted by a local calling from the back, "Don't come here telling us about snow!" Their expertise would come in handy when they traveled to voice their objections at the public hearing.

As the president, his wife, and several members of the committee set off for Sacramento, it began to snow—hard. They zipped past Carson Pass and Echo Summit, assuming that I-80 over Donner Summit would be their best bet. Just before the summit, they were stopped by CHP and told that the roadway was closed. The little band jumped out of their Ford and began to plead their case. They were experienced Eastern Sierrans and could handle themselves in a blizzard. Plus they were on an important mission to testify in Sacramento against a new trans-Sierra highway. At that, the officers relented but told them that if they got into trouble, they shouldn't expect a rescue. The intrepid group set off, cautiously descending the icy asphalt and stopping periodically to clear the windshield. The next day, still full of adrenalin, they joined Judge Sherwin and Genny Smith who carried a giant poster that laid out the key issues of the highway proposal.

On the day of the hearing, Genny placed her poster on an easel where it remained during the entire day. She had hired an architect to sketch out the elevations of Donner Summit and superimpose the even more severe elevation changes of the proposed highway. Her poster also included the costs of construction, maintenance, and snow removal based on the highway division's numbers. After testimony by representatives from the Mammoth Town Council, Chamber of Commerce, and Mono County Board of Supervisors, the committee, which included future US Senator Pete Wilson, over-whelmingly voted down the bill. Wilson voted no. The *Sacramento Bee* opined that the committee members had shown their indifference to the needs of Central California. Furious, the bill's sponsoring assemblyman announced that he would put forward a new bill "likely sooner than later."

Preemptively, as 1967 progressed, resources secretary Livermore scheduled meetings with government representatives to assess the best strategy to defeat the highway once and for all. One forester told him bluntly that the issue would persist as long as the designated corridor remained open. Another forester called FH 100 "the most important unconstructed road in California." Yet another brought an ironic "Minaret Summit Freeway" sign to an on-site visit. The sign declared, "Your highway taxes at work." Livermore tried to be a good sport, but for him it was no joke. Behind the scenes, he developed a proposal for Governor Reagan to put before the federal government: the state would relinquish land for a Redwood National Park if the federal government would give the Devils Postpile National Monument and surrounding wilderness, including the highway corridor, to California. He also organized a pack trip in the fall for foresters, conservationists, state officials, and reporters to ride the corridor and raise awareness of the wild nature of the area. A writer for the *Sacramento Union* called it "Ike Livermore's Wilderness Summit."

When Sisk found out about the proposal and the pack trip, he lost his cool. He accused Livermore of running a pack trip for public relations purposes and of a conflict of interest because of his ownership of a pack station. "Does Livermore speak for the Department of Transportation?" he asked. "It's time for the governor to express himself on the topic." He would hear from the governor, but the message would not be what he hoped for.

Sure enough, a new bill winged around in 1968. This one, virtually indistinguishable from the last one, would confer highway status on seventy-eight miles that lay between the two forest roads. The documents made no mention of the previous bill or the highway division report. Within two weeks, legislative analysts pointed out the similarity to the previous bill, noted the differences in cost estimates, and commented that the project was "completely objectionable to conservationists."

The John Muir Trail Association gathered forces, and letters began to arrive on committee members' desks. Mono County, Inyo County, Tuolumne County, and the California Council for Trout Unlimited voiced their opposition. Livermore issued a statement, declaring, "In this great state of ours where we have the largest population, the most prosperous and advanced industries, the richest agricultural valley, the highest mountain, the noblest redwoods, the most spectacular and beautiful state and national parks, we should also maintain intact the country's finest wilderness."

Nevertheless, two surprising events set a different stage this time for the committee's review. In 1953, Dave McCoy had received his first permit from the US Forest Service to operate the Mammoth Mountain ski area. After the lease was signed, the road up to Minaret Summit was minimally paved to provide access to the first lift and warming hut. As the popularity of the sport spread and more people, including Hollywood types, made the journey from Southern California, the state department of transportation rerouted SR 203 to improve access to the ski resort. Instead of continuing straight up Lake Mary Road, it now turned right at Minaret Road and climbed up to a dead end at Minaret Summit. This action had pulled five more miles of the proposed trans-Sierra crossing into the state highway system, thereby weakening the argument that a pristine wilderness should be preserved from more pavement.

The John Muir Trail Association was also startled when Ansel Adams switched sides and sent a letter in support of the highway advocates. His letter pronounced Minaret Summit the "least important and least interesting pass in the entire Sierra Nevada." As a person who snowshoes up to that summit at every opportunity, where I can gape at the Minarets, I find this statement so astonishing that I can only assume Adams had been hit very hard on the head before he wrote that letter. He went on to say that if such a crossing had been built years before, "we would have been spared the tragic invasion of the so-called improved road across Yosemite." Not only is that proclamation historically suspect, it smacks of sour grapes. Regardless, with that kind of adversary, the committee braced itself for a fight.

Republican sponsor Mobley was in charge of collecting the seven required votes for the bill, but he had trouble getting even a quorum present, not to mention a majority vote. Committee members wandered in and out during testimony, bored with hearing the same arguments again. Mobley had to keep asking for postponements to defer the vote. The *Fresno Bee* reported on the developments and quoted Mobley saying it was like "trying to hold onto a roomful of feathers in a strong wind." After debate ended with no vote called for, Mobley asked for another delay—and six months later the bill was defunct. This time, the highway advocates went quietly, and no threats were made about the introduction of further legislation.

The citizens of Mammoth Lakes heaved a sigh of relief and celebrated a significant victory. In their minds, ding dong, the road was dead. Imagine their surprise when in 1970 a group of not-to-be-named mothers and kids were exploring on the forest road down to Reds Meadow and discovered surveyors' stakes marking sections where the roadbed would be widened. In a display of good old outlaw Mammoth Lakes spirit, the kids and mothers pulled up the markers, ripped out the yellow marking tape, snapped the stakes in two, and threw the whole kit and caboodle into the forest gully. The record would later show that despite the decision taken at the state level, federal funds had been approved to make modest improvements to the road, and a surveying contract had been awarded. Delayed by the citizens' actions, termed "civil disobedience" by the locals and "vandalism" by the US Forest Service, the project was soon covered by winter snow and came to a halt.

Two years later, tipped off by a report in the Bridgeport newspaper, Livermore became aware that the US Forest Service was again seeking improvements to FH 100. The National Park Service believed the current passage was too hazardous and wanted a two-lane road down to Devils Postpile. Livermore, who believed visitors should walk or take a mule, wrote to remind those involved that the state didn't want the road and that such proposals should be run by his office. In the ensuing exchange of letters, the feds basically told Livermore to go pound sand. They intended to reconstruct what represented a portion of the trans-Sierra road and refused to confirm that the rest of the highway would not be built. By April 1972, $1.6 million had been appropriated to widen the road from Minaret Summit to Devils Postpile and another $790,000 to extend the paved road as far as Reds Meadow. Livermore now knew he would have to take the fight to Washington.

His first move was to draft several letters objecting to the project for Reagan to send to the US Department of Transportation secretary with whom Reagan was on a first-name basis. The secretary's delayed and surprised response maintained that the current road was judged to be hazardous, the proposed improvements were reasonable, and those improvements would come at no expense to California. He added that the feds had generously allocated $100 million more to California for roads in 1972 than it had in 1971. He missed the point, to say the least. With the secretaries of the interior and agriculture presumably also on board with the improvement project, Livermore and Reagan now had three cabinet secretaries set against them. Livermore decided to take it up a notch and go to the president.

Governor Reagan and President Nixon were not friends. They had crossed swords over the 1968 Republican presidential nomination when Reagan tried but failed to oust Nixon from the ticket, and they were further alienated when Nixon chose Spiro Agnew over Reagan as his running mate. Reagan did, however, have a Washington ally in Caspar Weinberger who had served as Reagan's finance director before moving to Washington to become a federal trade commissioner. Known as a cheapskate, he would later engage in so much cost cutting at the White House that he would earn the nickname "Cap the Knife." Canceling a $2.4 million construction project would be right up his alley. A warm exchange between the two men began.

At that time, both Reagan and Nixon could have used some positive conservation public relations. Nixon had created the EPA, but had otherwise shown little interest in the environment. Reagan had become a target for conservationist ire after he complained about all the hubbub over the redwoods, allegedly saying, "You've seen one redwood, you've seen them all." His defenders objected to the quote because what he actually said was, "If you've looked at a hundred thousand acres or so of trees—you know, a tree is a tree; how many more do you need to look at?" which strikes me as only different in numeric scope. He made this statement at a Wood Products Manufacturers Association meeting, no less. One of his most significant acts on behalf of the environment was to appoint Livermore as his resources secretary. That appointment was about to pay off.

Weinberger recognized the political opportunity Reagan had handed him and drafted a statement for the president cancelling the funds for the road, thereby saving some money and enhancing his environmental record in one fell swoop. Weinberger suggested that the statement be announced by the governor and the secretary of the interior the following week, scooping a scheduled Sierra Club press conference planned to call out the administration for its destruction of the wilderness.

On June 22, 1972, he forwarded the statement and a cover note to John Ehrlichman, assistant for domestic affairs. Nixon himself was busy that day, attending a press conference at which he issued his first official denial of any White House involvement with the recent burglary of the Democratic National Committee Headquarters in the Watergate office complex. Weinberger's cover note evokes an uneasy nostalgia as he copied Ron Ziegler, Bob Haldeman, and John Mitchell, names that those of us of a certain age recall with a slight shiver. Weinberger asked in the cover memo if Ehrlichman had "a problem" with releasing the statement.

We have no record of what went through Ehrlichman's mind when he considered this request, so I can only speculate. It's possible he was distracted by the prevailing events. It's also possible he was genuinely supportive; he was a Californian after all, he had nearly twenty years of experience as a land-use attorney, and he had supported environmental efforts when he lived in Seattle. Whatever the reason—he penciled in the margin, "No problem," changing the future of our little town forever.

Now armed with the biggest weapon of his career, Livermore was determined to maximize the drama and public relations potential of an event at which his boss would announce the heroic rescue of the Sierra. He rushed to organize a two-day pack trip during which guests would ride out to Summit Meadow, camp, and attend a press conference in a gorgeous natural location with a view of the mountains. Invitations for June 27 were issued to agency representatives, elected officials, and, of course, reporters.

When Bob and Jean Tanner, owners of the Reds Meadow Pack Station heard that sixty luminaries were bearing down on them expecting horses, mules, food, tents, and riding gear, they turned to Rock Creek Pack Station for additional stock and provisions. The day before the guests arrived, they also called on Lou Roeser at Mammoth Lakes Pack Outfit for more horses. In typical Mammoth style, the locals snapped into action to pull off a party that would wow even the governor. Jean Tanner would say later that they weren't starstruck because they were accustomed to providing stock and gear to the Hollywood elite for movie shoots. As it would turn out, she was the only woman allowed on the trip; instructions had been given that this was to be an all-guy event.

While some of the reporters were not thrilled to have to ride a horse to attend a press conference, Reagan was more than game. An experienced horseman, he dressed in a cowboy hat and shirtsleeves and was seated on a pretty chestnut mare named Lady. He thoroughly enjoyed the ride, ignoring the consternation of his security detail who were unable to fan out behind him but were relegated to riding single file along the pack trail. To the amusement of the packers, the agents consoled themselves by riding with their rifles held in ready position, alert for any wild man or thing that might jump out of the forest.

The trip was not without mishaps. Some of the reporters dismounted to scramble up the switchbacks and attempt to photograph the governor, blocking the trail and confusing the horses. One reporter lost his footing and dropped his camera down a ravine. The novices struggled to remount on the rocky trail. Lee Roeser, Lou's teenage son, was assigned to the photographers and attempted to restore order by helping the stragglers back on their horses so they would not miss the event.

After they arrived at Summit Meadow, a high pasture with a 360-degree view of the mountains, the guests enjoyed sandwiches and sodas before Reagan gathered them around an easel that held a map of the proposed highway. He provided background on the proposal and his history of opposing it, as well as his objection to building what he called a "high-speed" passage to Devils Postpile. It would, he said, "represent a foot in the door to those intent on paving yet another road across the Sierra." He then reached into his pocket for his coup de grâce, a telegram from the president. He read, "The president announced today that the proposed reconstruction of a portion of the Minarets Highway in California will not be undertaken, and the proposed Trans-Sierra Highway (FH 100) will not be built... The president said that the environmental considerations and the need to preserve the atmosphere and ecology of the Sierra region of California clearly overrode the other factors that had been urged in supporting the construction proposals."

The press reacted with extensive coverage, not only of the president's action, but of the dramatic announcement in a spectacular location. Local papers praised the event planners and all those involved. Years later, *Los Angeles Times* political columnist George Skelton called it the "greatest political photo op ever," and referred to Reagan as a "right-winger who unexpectedly became the savior of the Sierra" and "a man waving a white hat as he led a pack train into the wilderness." Fact checkers would claim that his hat was silver, not white, but it looks dang white in the photographs.

And where was the guy behind the event, Ike Livermore, who had spent years laying the foundation for this significant victory? At the request of the White House, he was attending a United Nations conference on the environment. He would say later, "I was stuck in Stockholm."

After news of the press conference had died down, pack station owner and highway opponent Bob Tanner was notified by the tax authorities of Madera County that he should prepare for an audit and appraisal of his property. In response, he fired off a letter asking whether he had been selected because Reagan and company had ridden his horses and asking if the county really thought he was powerful enough to stop a road. He never received a response and the auditors never arrived, perhaps because of the hassle of auditing someone who didn't live near a road. Reagan was more appreciative and wrote a long letter to Tanner that expressed his thanks for the "hurculean [sic] effort" in organizing the press conference. He also asked that Tanner give Lady his regards.

The *Fresno Bee* did not relish the news of the Summit Meadow announcement and pointed out that the corridor still existed between two protected wilderness areas, which left open the possibility that a highway could eventually be built. An advocate said, "Congress has decreed that part of the Sierra not be included in the wilderness area, so it will take more than a president and a governor's order to change it." Reagan himself warned those celebrating that more action was needed to "prevent the creation of a high-speed trans-Sierra highway through this area for all time." Indeed Sisk sent a scathing letter to Reagan accusing the governor of denying California citizens what was rightfully theirs with a publicity stunt. He also referred to the corridor, writing, "I do not know how far your pony took you... but I am sure you must have noticed a great difference between the character of the corridor itself and the Minarets."

Between 1972 and 1978, the highway opponents remained alert for any developments and continued their letter-writing efforts to squash any advancements. They were taken by surprise, however, by the regrading of the road from Minaret Summit down to Agnew Meadows, which the *Fresno Bee* gleefully reported as costing a mere $51,000. Then in 1975, the *Bee* reported that $1.5 million had been awarded to the US Forest Service to improve forty-three miles of the forest highway out of North Fork, at the other end of the proposed crossing. Livermore, Judge Sherwin, and Genny Smith exchanged letters complaining of "funny business." It was time to try to close the corridor.

The north boundary of the corridor was formed by the Minarets Wilderness area that butted up against Yosemite National Park. To the south lay the John Muir Wilderness area. The areas had been so designated by the 1964 Wilderness Act signed into law by President Johnson after seven years of bartering and endless testimony. It was rewritten and reintroduced to Congress sixty-six times. Although it finally passed by a landslide, preservationists were disappointed that the sixty million acres the bill was originally intended to protect dwindled to only nine million, partly because of lobbying by the US Forest Service who sought to retain the land under their jurisdiction. The National Park Service opposed the bill in its entirety and argued that the parks provided enough wilderness for Americans. In 1978, President Carter signed into law the Endangered American Wilderness Act which added sixteen million acres to the total, but every wilderness expansion was fraught with controversy. Congressional approval would be required to expand a wilderness area to include the 159,000 acres in the corridor. Reagan turned to California Democratic Senator Alan Cranston to get the ball rolling.

Sisk and the citizens of Fresno and Madera Counties also moved into action. They recognized that the designation of the corridor as wilderness would spell an end to the possibility of a crossing. They were joined by lumbering and mining interests, as the highway opponents expected. They then became aware of an unanticipated potential threat from a powerful local constituency when the ski area released its master plan. The plan called for the development of the back side of the mountain, the installation of eight new lifts, and the addition of 582 acres of ski runs smack in the middle of the corridor. Genny Smith got in touch with Dave McCoy, owner of the ski area, and asked for his support of the wilderness bill. She argued that the snow on that side of the mountain, facing south and west, would be less plentiful and of poor quality. She was delighted when McCoy's son responded to an inquiry by the Bureau of Public Roads by saying that the ski area would not object to the wilderness designation if it came to fruition. The Mammoth contingent heaved a sigh of relief that the mighty McCoy would not stand in their way.

Cranston teamed up with Phil Burton, a California Democratic Congressman and former mayor of San Francisco who had served eleven terms and was known as a strong advocate for the wilderness. Livermore, Judge Sherwin, and Genny Smith all appeared before the house committee in support of their first legislative effort. Genny still carried her old poster depicting the challenges presented by the crossing's geography and how much higher it was than I-80 over Donner Summit. The bill that designated 3.5 million additional acres as wilderness, including the corridor's 153,000 acres, was presented in 1981. It passed in the House, but the Senate version, introduced by Cranston, failed. Cranston and Burton regrouped and prepared to introduce a revised version in 1983. Sadly, Phil Burton was taken out of the battle when he passed away suddenly from thrombosis.

Cranston asked fellow Republican Senator Pete Wilson for support. Wilson had been a member of the transportation committee that rejected Sisk's efforts to get the trans-Sierra highway built and remembered the issues well. The two developed a bill to designate 3.2 million acres as additional California wilderness and to add the corridor, now reduced to 119,000 acres, to the Minarets Wilderness. Movers and shakers from Fresno and Madera Counties pressed on with their objections on the basis of mining, year-round access, national defense, tourism, etc. Opposition to "Phil Burton's Bill," as it was still known, even came from the White House, now occupied by President Reagan, who felt that the bill was too broad.

The bill passed both houses, the president signed it into law in September 1984, and the corridor was officially joined to the Minarets Wilderness. To the astonishment of the locals, the area was renamed the Ansel Adams Wilderness, presumably because of the influence of the Wilderness Society's executive director who was a good friend of Adams. Soon all the trailheads in the former corridor would be adorned by signs bearing the name of a man who had described the area as unimportant and uninteresting. Name-calling aside, the 211 miles of the John Muir Trail, the longest stretch of trail unbroken by roads in the lower forty-eight, were now protected.

When my son and I started preparing for spring break and how he would once again navigate the mountain barrier, I thought of the people who caused this inconvenience: Ike Livermore and Judge Sherwin, Bob and Jean Tanner, Bob and Peggy Schotz, Lou and Marye Roeser, Tom Dempsey, and Genny Smith with her twenty-seven years of letter writing, A big thank you to you all. I appreciate the trouble.

LOCAL FAUNA

*The Felici Piano Trio impresses with captivating vitality
and impulsivity, perfection without aloofness.*

~ GERMAN NEWSPAPER REVIEW

September 29–October 5, 2014
Monday

*I DREAM THAT someone in the neighborhood owns a tiger. As I watch
him walk by on the street, sporting a bandanna around his neck, I
think, "You should put that in your journal. People will want to know
about **that**."*

Our first hard frost came last night, and the flowers and bushes
were lit with sparkles this morning. Mammoth Mountain has a good
sprinkling of snow, and the western slopes of the White Mountains
are now actually white. We put on more layers; even Julian added a
windbreaker as a concession to the thirty-three degree temperature.
It warmed up during the day, and by the time soccer practice rolled
around, it was practically balmy. And the forecast is for a return to
summer temperatures by the end of the week. Nevertheless, I think
we have been warned.

Tuesday

A five-deer day today: a doe and fawn on Old Mammoth Road, and then three hiding in the shade of a tree down in Sherwin Meadows. Taking advantage of a pickup by car in town, I hiked the Panorama Dome-Mammoth Rock trail to enjoy the beauty and variety of the scenery in the forest. I emerged in the foothills and followed the dusty roads back to the school. The meadows hidden behind the trees before you reach the flatlands are so full of flowers and birds, I felt like Heidi of the Swiss Alps and imagined myself accompanied by goats.

I drove Tom, Julian, and Oscar up to Minaret Vista so that they could ride down the Mountain View and Downtown mountain bike trails and on to town to celebrate what may be our last warm temperatures and also a day without soccer practice.

Wednesday

On the ride home from baseball practice, Julian tells the other boys about seeing a little old lady speeding down US 395 in an enormous extended-cab pickup.

"Across the back of it, it said **TEXAS**," he chuckles.

The talk turns to the teachers. It turns out there's a baffling array of Mrs. Wiesner, Ms. Wizzer, and Ms. Wisher. And that Mrs. Vanko's daughter also taught at the school and is "so cool." Taff complains at length that the Math teacher only calls on people she likes and *never* calls on him even though he always has the right answer just because one time she did call on him and his answer was a tiny bit off because he had multiplied something wrong and so now she won't call on him at all.

"It's not *fair*," he says.

"It's not like it matters, dude. It doesn't affect your grade or anything," Will tries to reason with him.

"It's not *that*. It's just that I want to give the *answer*," Taff retorts.

"Why? No one cares," Will says.

"It matters to *me*. I just want to, that's all," Taff says and slumps into a mournful silence. Later he perks up and tells us about a time he threw a tennis racket at his sister.

"Which one?" asks Julian.

"*Both* of them," says Taff.

"Why?" asks Will. "Did they not call on you?"

Thursday

As neighborhoods in Mammoth Lakes have aged, their relative value has decreased and they have become more affordable to the local residents. When I first started coming here, the houses surrounding the family's house on Majestic Pines Drive were all second homes and usually empty. Now that twenty years have passed, nearly half of the houses in this neighborhood are occupied by permanent residents.

You can identify the second homes by the occasional foreign car parked daintily in the driveway, while the locals park their trucks and cars and trailers and snowblowers willy-nilly across their yards. Now that we have two cars and the dead Subaru all parked in the front yard, we could pass for people who live here, especially if we put a sign on the Subaru that says: "FOR SALE. $300 OBO."

Not so with the development on the distant other end of Majestic Pines. It is new, and those houses and condos are all empty, with only an occasional landscaper to be seen. I was hiking through that empty condo complex this afternoon and came across something unusual on the bike path: a small deer leg with hoof intact—the crudely broken

199

foreleg from a fawn. The flesh had been scraped from several inches of exposed bone. The rest of the body was missing. While picturing what led to this remnant of violence, I became aware of how quiet it was. *Was someone or* some thing *watching me?* A cool breeze came up, raising the hair on the back of my neck and I scurried home.

Friday
A woman hailed me on my hike today. "Beautiful fall colors!" she exclaimed, gesturing at the hillside.

"Mm, pretty," I agreed. But like a good Hoosier, I was thinking, *Look, lady. I'll give you your panoramas, indigo skies, joyful mountain meadows, and pristine lakes. But fall colors? Bah. That's just a yellow bush.*

We played baseball with Taff after school, in seventy-one degree weather and brought him home for pool and a movie. On the way, he announced that his dad was out hunting: "Him and his friend were driving yesterday? And three deer ran across the road in front of them. And I'm like, just hit them! There, hunt's *over*. Or just lean out and shoot them—that to me would be more exciting." Not quite the typical Mammoth sportsman.

Saturday
The temperature this morning was over seventy degrees—hard to believe it's October. We grabbed Taff this morning and set out to complete the last of the required hikes for middle school PE. We chose Sherwin Lakes Trail, a three-mile hike departing from a meadow beside Sherwin Creek Road and climbing 1,000 feet up to a lovely small shallow lake. It offered tremendous views back over the town, countless switchbacks through large Jeffrey pines, and an interesting section where the aspens appeared to have panicked (perhaps because

of a fire) and thrown all their branches down on the ground creating a graveyard of white tree bones. We also saw several trees that had been completely stripped of their bark that was lying around them in piles of slabs, triggering speculation about bear activity. Don't believe everything you read on the Internet, but *it* says that black bears strip the bark off trees in the spring to eat the new sugary wood underneath and that one bear can strip seventy trees a day.

We enjoyed the views and the picturesque lake as fast as we could since we needed to get to Julian's soccer game on time. The boys entertained us with jokes of the "a man walked into a bar—and fell down" variety. We were only a little bit late to "warm-ups" on one of the hottest days of the season. It seemed inconceivable that it was so cold only one week ago. The boys played well; better attendance at practice seems to be paying off, and the team was organized and in control most of the game. They won 2–0, their first victory, and the score would have been higher were it not for some near misses. Coach Alex scheduled the promised pizza party for tomorrow.

The only dark moment of the game was how put out one of the soccer moms was when her ex showed up from out of town with no advance notice.

"This is so disrespectful," she fumed. "He could have texted me."

"Do you want me to go punch him?" Tom asked, joking.

"Yes!" she said, not joking.

Tom looked alarmed.

A few weeks ago, I was chatting with one of the soccer moms; nearby a dad was putting on green soccer socks in preparation to be sideline ref. I noticed him because a few days before I had seen him vault over the fence to retrieve an errant ball. While he finished "suiting up," I mentioned that I was from Southern Indiana. His head came up. *Ho-ho,* I thought, *Something is up with that.* Sure enough, he ambled over.

"Where are you from in Indiana?" he asked.

"Bloomington," I said.

His face lit up. "I went to school there!" he said. "We loved Bloomington. We were at the School of Music."

"You WERE?" I said. "That's a very good school."

"Yes, I play cello, and my wife plays violin," he said.

Then I realized who he was. I had read about the chamber music trio in town, comprised of a husband and wife from Mammoth Lakes plus a pianist from LA. I had *not* expected to run into them on the soccer field.

And that is how I found myself in the atrium of the community college this evening listening to two Indiana-University-Jacobs-School-of-Music-trained musicians and an internationally renowned pianist play Schubert for a fee of twenty dollars. They are the Felici Piano Trio; its members are Belgian pianist Steven Vanhauwaert, German violinist Rebecca Hang, and American cellist Brian Schuldt. They no longer looked like soccer parents—Brian had lost his green socks, and Rebecca's introduction of the pieces exhibited her musical knowledge and ease in front of an audience. The professionalism of all three was evident, and the superb playing signaled they are the real deal.

This was the first concert of the trio's 17th annual season, and the music was fantastic. They opened with a piece for violin and cello by Ermanno Wolf-Ferrari (what a great name) who, the performers explained, mixed up elements from his Italian and German heritages to create a piece that was just a bit off-kilter. They then played a piano trio by a composer I had never heard of, Ernest Chausson, a little-known contemporary and friend of Debussy's. It was absolutely marvelous and the highlight of the evening. They finished with all four movements of an old friend, Schubert's piano trio in B-flat major.

About two hundred people attended, almost all over the age of sixty-five. They did not look like People Who Live Here, so I suspect they were People Who Have Retired Here. There was a very small handful of children, including Julian. He said the performance was very good.

Their next concert is November 1, and they will add a viola. What a wonderful evening.

Sunday

This morning, I succeeded in making Swedish pancakes, and we ate them out on the deck in the warm sunshine. Now, we are truly settled.

We spent the morning working on getting the Subaru started— and we did! It put out a lot of smoke at first, but the engine ran smoothly. I recounted our success to one of the baseball moms later in the day and told her that it "only" has 116,000 miles on it, despite dating from 1993.

"That's nothing!" she said, "My Subaru had 260,000 miles on it. You should keep that car!" Kristen was adamant. "You're going to want that car."

Planning for dinner, I said to Tom, "We could have a nice evening at home."

"Yeah. Or we could fight," he offered.

October 6–12, 2014

Monday

After school we rode along Knolls Loop Trail in Shady Rest, an elevated single track through the trees that parallels the paved road.

It leaves the park near an aging A-frame that, as a boy, Tom and his parents stayed in during one trip long ago. Tom said, "It never occurred to me that one day I would be riding past that house on a mountain bike with my wife... partly because mountain bikes hadn't been invented yet."

There's a story in the paper about a guy who discovered a bear inside a dumpster and *locked it in*. Then he called the police.

"I caught one!" the nitwit kept saying to the people who had gathered around to watch.

When the police ordered him to let the bear out, he refused, indicating he still had a few brain cells left because—judging by the slamming and banging from within the dumpster—the bear now was infuriated. So the cops ordered everyone to leave and then released the poor bear.

I got carded at the liquor store. Something up here must be agreeing with me. Or the clerk is blind in one eye. Which is more likely.

Tuesday

After the Mammoth Mountain Bike Park closes, the locals are allowed to ride on the trails for free. With winter creeping up on us, we took advantage of the continued warm weather and went out for a mountain bike ride after school. Tom mapped a long single-track route that goes all the way from Minaret Summit down to our house, traversing the entire front of the mountain, across Chair 12, Broadway, the Mill, Chair 21, the Art Park, Canyon Express, and finally on to Chair 15. It's an amazing ride, like an extended version of the Twilight Zone ski trail, with banked turns in the forest, bumps over tree roots, tunnels under the Kamikaze boardwalks, sandy S turns down the steep parts, and open-air dusty straightaways across the face of the ski runs. Riding across the Bridges Ski Run, we discovered a young deer hastily eating a bush as though it were about to be taken away from him. He was so busy, he hardly glanced at us.

The trail approaches Lake Mary Road below Twin Lakes and then turns back down toward town. It parallels the road until you ride up the lip of the ski run under Chair 15, go through a series of bricked banked curves, cross the bridge, and dive down Voodoo Chute to the campground and our house. It was two hours of SO MUCH FUN—and I only fell over once. When we got in the door, Julian said, "Favorite trail. Right there."

Dodgeball season has started, and the paper ran several photos of locals smacking each other with red balls. The city league is still looking for one more team of eight, if that sounds entertaining. It only costs sixty-eight dollars to join. The ad for the games shows a person fallen over backwards with only his sticking-up feet visible and several balls lying around him. The paper says it's "fun as hell."

Thursday

Yesterday on my hike, I found an entire fawn body. Disappointingly, it had been struck by a car on Lake Mary Road, and its small body was less than a mile from the sign that says, "Speeding Kills Wildlife."

Today on my hike, a pickup was waiting at an intersection as I approached. Just as the driver looked at me, someone on my podcast said something funny and I burst out laughing. The driver leaned over and gave me a long look through the window before he waved and pulled out. It occurred to me that since I was carrying some empty beer cans I had picked up, he might have thought I was drunk.

I didn't think it would help clarify the situation though if I called out, "I'm not drunk!"

Last week, Tom biked from Minaret Summit down to Stark-weather Lake, a drop of 1,000 feet and then *rode back up*, which is nuts. As a trail ride, it's only permissible briefly in the spring and the fall, which may be a good thing for the health of our local cyclists. In today's wind, he went on a *six*-hour bike ride and rode to the top of Mammoth Mountain and back, an ascent and descent of about 3,000 feet. He was cold and nearly sick by the time he got back. But he made it.

Friday

The golf courses close this weekend, and we are officially in shoulder season. The town is very quiet, and few cars are on the roads. One car stopped in the middle of Main Street the other day so that the people crossing the street could pet the dog in the car. The newspaper ran an article called "The big empty" about this time of year. Some restaurants are offering half-off lunches, and some businesses just close until Thanksgiving, like Brian's Bicycles & Cross-Country Skis. When Brian comes back, his shop will transform from a bike shop to a ski shop. Kristen said I was going to like it here now "when it's just us locals."

Small town events: yesterday, the woman who checked out my books for me at the library said, "I saw you at the concert!"

As I was getting the newspapers from the boxes in front of Domino's Pizza (yes, there is a Domino's here), a friendly man came up to get his papers, and we exchanged pleasantries. I ran into him at Vons later that day when he called up the aisle to his wife, "**Is toilet paper the last thing you have to get?**" and then turned to me after a beat and said, "No answer." Then he recognized me and introduced himself as Franken, "like Frankenstein," and inquired about our move up here. "You've been coming up here for years, haven't you, and now you've finally decided to move. Good for you," he said. He was very welcoming.

I notice that, as part of a small community, you feel more responsibility for its well-being, like being more careful to put the shopping cart away securely because you wouldn't want it to roll away and hit someone. I had picked up a plastic bag that was blowing around the bike path, and a woman passed me on her bike and called back over her shoulder, "I was going to pick that up." Perhaps that is why the locals just *freeze*—even if we don't have the right of way—when we approach an intersection on bicycles, especially when Julian is with us.

The sad events are sadder too. Last Sunday afternoon, a young English woman was killed riding on the back of a motorcycle driven by a drunk Mammoth Lakes man. The police said that alcohol and excessive speed contributed to the accident. The two crashed a few blocks from our house on Meridian in front of the Summit Condominiums, where one of Julian's schoolmates lives. The English woman was here on a four-month work visa and was due to return to London in eight days. Apparently she had accepted a ride home from a customer at the bar where she worked. Kristen said wisely, "In Mammoth, you can always just walk home. *Just walk.*" Tom pointed out later that the road design is unusual in that the curve tightens the deeper into it you get; the usual design starts at its tightest and gradually opens up, allowing those who drive like race car drivers, like my mother, to "accelerate into the curve," as she would say. If you accelerate into that curve on Meridian, you end up in our friends' driveway, just as the motorcycle driver did.

Death seems to come easily here. A young man from Arizona fell to his death while rock climbing solo. Earlier that day, he had proposed to his girlfriend and told her when she accepted, "This is the happiest day of my life." A twenty-seven-year-old Mammoth Lakes man drowned last month while swimming across Grant Lake. Last year, a popular twenty-nine-year-old Colorado transplant, known for partying, was found dead in a Jacuzzi. A well-liked local man, forty-three years of age, suffering from thyroid cancer, apparently threw himself into the Sacramento River and drowned. A few years ago, after an evening of heavy drinking, a teenager simply expired during the night.

Just being at altitude is dangerous for some people, especially those with heart conditions. One study showed that skiing at altitude is one of the most strenuous things that otherwise sedentary, middle-aged men do. A local family practitioner said that some people "just shouldn't be here in the first place." Snowboard coach Pete del'Giudice (he's the guy who discovered Olympic gold medalist Kelly Clark) said in an interview with *Mammoth Monthly* way back in 2003 that the biggest challenge to the ski industry was health and that people were skiing less because they *couldn't*, they just weren't fit enough.

A contributing factor to the deaths is that people are active here, so accidental deaths of young people are more common. I also keep noticing how many of the middle school students are on crutches or have casts on their arms or legs. "There's another one," I whispered to Tom the other day as a girl walked by with a cast on her ankle.

"Do you think it's part of Understanding Differences?" he said, referring to a disability awareness program at the Del Mar school that attempts to instill empathy in elementary school children for people who are blind, deaf, or otherwise disabled or "different." Nope, I think they're just active. Older people are active too; it's amazing how many bikes there are on the parents' cars at soccer and baseball.

After Terry Gooch Ross' protagonist in the novel *A Twin Falls* is injured in an airplane accident, she wonders, *Who in town could possibly look this beaten up?* She writes, "Then I remembered that I live in a ski resort town, where cuts, bruises, and broken bones are part of the local color."

Saturday

We were asked to participate in a fundraiser for the baseball team this morning. In addition to the money the team earns washing windows and cars, the owner of the Chevron station will donate ten cents for every gallon of gas sold today to put new red clay on the infield. So, in another of those scenes where I think to myself, *How did I get here?* Julian and I found ourselves standing on Main Street, holding up paper signs encouraging people to "Support Mammoth Sports" and "FILL UP!" The station was extremely busy while we were there; either our efforts were very effective, or everyone gets gas on Saturday morning. It was an active scene: boys in their Mammoth Huskies jerseys chatting, washing windows, and running the sprayers in the car wash. One baseball dad gave the boys a tutorial on the correct way to wash windows, but when the boys took over, the results were fairly imperfect. Nevertheless, people were enthusiastic, even the out-of-towners, and lots of people donated cash on the spot. The green Forest Service truck came by and BLASTED their horn for us.

Now we're not just fighting bears—we're fighting over bears.

One night, a young couple broke up. The man agreed to give the woman a ride to the bus stop the next morning, and she packed her luggage in the car. In the morning they discovered that a bear had broken in through a window and strewn her belongings around. The man accused the woman of packing a bag of chips in her luggage and causing the break-in, and the police intervened when a shoving match developed. No charges were filed, and the police gave her a ride to the bus station after she repacked her bags.

Sunday

A few weeks ago, after our new neighbors had moved in, I found an assortment of plastic Easter eggs and little girl's jewelry, an Anakin figure complete with light saber, an R2–D2, and a smashed wind-up bunny rabbit in our yard. *Did a boy in some passing car throw his sister's toys out the window? Why is the bunny crushed? Did someone drive over it?* After wondering about this for several days, I brought them inside and washed the salvageable items in the dishwasher. Today, I took them over to the new neighbors to see if the toys belonged to them. Yes, they did. The night they were moving in, an Easter basket containing some chocolate eggs was left outside. Along came a mother bear and a baby bear, and the mother took off with the Easter basket in her mouth! I did not find any chocolate eggs, so they must have polished those off. So there's an explanation for everything, and up here the explanation is usually: because bears.

The baseball coaches barbecued hot dogs for the boys and their families down at Whitmore this afternoon. They hoisted a large outdoor grill onto a truck, drove it down there, roasted about eighty hot dogs, and served them up with little fanfare. Teenage boys can eat an impressive number of hot dogs.

October 13–19, 2014
Monday

We discovered a family photo from Thanksgiving 2004 of snow piled high in the campground across the street. At Christmas that year, Tom's sister and brother-in-law built an igloo, and my mother made snow angels in the driveway. There was so much snow! The weather's going to have to change fast to recreate that this year.

The town has snapped into action with construction projects going on all over town: they're putting a sidewalk on Meridian, they have dug up the sewer on lower Majestic Pines, and they're working on one of the bridges on the bike path. The Mountain also is in maintenance mode; everywhere trucks and staff are working on the lifts and standing around staring at equipment. Last week on his bike ride, Tom saw a worker put a ladder *on the chair* of the highest lift on the mountain and balance it against the cable above in order to climb up to do something to the cable. Can you imagine being up there on that thing swinging around?

Wednesday

Tom and I gathered up soccer equipment, food, drinks, chairs, clothing, and two other families and drove down to Whitmore to collect Julian from baseball practice for a 7:30 p.m. soccer game in Bishop. As we set off with a glorious sunset behind us and headed into the dusk, it felt as though we were embarking on a road trip and the party van was abuzz with excitement. The game was behind Carl's Jr. on an unmarked field with sketchy lighting, but the game was painful enough that we were thankful for the gloom. Afterwards, we hurried the kids into the car and back into their beds as soon as possible, but it was nearly 10:00 p.m. before they were asleep.

On the way home, the parents told snow stories. One was about a girl who left her car and froze to death going for help in a blizzard after she and her mother had attempted to get up to Mammoth by an alternate route because Sherwin Grade was closed. ("Don't leave your car," our companions warned us.) Another story was about one mother's struggle to get over Carson Pass in a snowstorm that was so bad the road closed immediately behind her. They chuckled about how *some people* carry empty tire chain boxes to point to and fool the highway patrol guys when they ask if there are chains in the car.

Thursday

Three rough-hewn, grizzled men ahead of me at Rite Aid were carrying what looked to be gallon-sized bottles of vodka and whiskey. The first was asked for his ID although he appeared to me to be at least sixty.

"You better card him good," a guy behind me called out and then spotting the other two, said, "Oh-ho. There's trouble!" The three men ahead of me invited him to stop by their get-together, but he declined, saying he was going "up the hill."

"I'm going for the prize," he said. "Last week I caught an eight-pound golden. 'Course, I let it go, so it isn't official."

"That's a nice trout," one of the other men said.

"Are you kidding me?" the guy behind me said. "That's an *awesome* fish. I think I'll win if I get a nine-pounder. 'Til then, I'll just do catch and release."

"That's the funnest part," the other man agreed. "Watching 'em swim away."

When I got to the counter, I asked if they carded everyone purchasing liquor.

"Pretty much," the clerk said.

"I took it as a compliment," I said. "Until I saw those guys."

He chuckled.

Saturday

Julian announced at two minutes to nine last night that there was a soccer game at eight this morning. "What?!" I yelled and ran upstairs to call Kristen.

"WHAT??!!" she yelled and went to get Oscar. He sort of confirmed this announcement although there was some vagueness about when we were supposed to get there. So, at seven thirty this morning, we were standing in the cold at Shady Rest looking at a deserted soccer field. Then Mac and Kristen and Oscar showed up. We were relieved when another mother drove up, but it turned out she was only there because Mac texted her. So far, all of us were there only on Julian's and Oscar's say-so. A soccer guy in red showed up but left. Then Steven's dad appeared and called out the car window, "Is someone pulling my leg?" He also joked, "Don't you know what AYSO stands for? All Your Saturdays Occupied."

Eventually the whole team did appear, and the opposing Red team arrived, and we did, in fact, have a soccer game. Which Yellow lost. It was the last game of the season, and all the parents were a bit mournful. The boys seemed unaffected.

Julian took an incredibly hard kick off his face (from the phenomenal kicker Lexis) when he was in the wall blocking a free kick. It did break his glasses but did not break his nose. He sat out briefly and then went back in. Tough kid. One of the sideline refs said he'd never seen anybody get hit that hard.

Tom's geologist sister and one of her colleagues came up for the weekend to sightsee, and we set off for Lundy Lake, about forty minutes away by car. Some people said in the paper it was their favorite hike, so I was excited to go. From the road, we could see the gorgeous fall colors and how they mark the creeks and waterways with orange and yellow wooly worms that crawl up the canyons. In other spots, a single orange tree beams from the dark stone, like a proud flare.

There is a lot of beaver activity above Lundy Lake, creating an extended series of dams and water passages surrounded by aspens, elders, and cottonwoods. Our visitors are bird nuts and taught us to listen for the birds. We saw a Townsend's solitaire, who had a beautiful song, and a red-tailed hawk who was hanging out on a dead tree waiting for some action. The hike took us across some shale outcroppings, through a grove of huge aspens extensively marked with graffiti, across more creeks and meadows, and finally up, up, up into the cliffs deep into the canyon with great views of water and flora.

We then dashed to Mono Lake to check out the last rays of sunshine on the water. The temperature was dropping, and Tom's sister got a hilarious photo of a puffed-up grebe with his face all squished up from the cold. Afterward, because this is what happens when you hang out with geologists, I found myself at nine at night, huddled in an enormous borrowed down jacket, staring up at the sky over Mono Lake in an attempt to see the rise of the Milky Way. The stars were spectacular, and our headlamps picked up a pair of green eyes in the bush staring at us. We speculated that they were the eyes of a fox, but Wikipedia says that they could have been a cat, a dog, or—you guessed it—a bear.

Sunday

We were up early for a baseball doubleheader *out of state*. Games were scheduled in Dayton, Nevada, near Carson City, about three hours away. The route to Carson City on US 395 turns out to be an extremely dangerous drive: a high-speed, curvy, hilly, two-lane road with deer lurking behind every bush. While we were driving, I happened to read about an eighteen-wheeler whose driver fell asleep, causing the truck to cross the lane of the oncoming cars and crash into Virginia Creek just in the area we were passing through. Last year, a big rig failed to negotiate a turn in Bridgeport, crashed into the East Walker River, and exploded, killing the driver. Yikes. I'm floored that people routinely make that drive. Kristen commuted there weekly for a year to hold down a nursing job. Still, it was beautiful with the fall colors along the river, where we stopped briefly at a rest stop. Nevada has some trees that turn a deep gorgeous red to add to the orange and yellow.

Since what you do in Carson City is shop, we did all the important things: got a battery for the Subaru, a costume for Julian at the Spirit Halloween store, and a new jacket for him at Walmart. And then we went to Trader Joe's where Tom bought pumpkin everything: cereal, bagels, Pop-Tarts, cake mix, corn bread mix, bars, cookies, pie mix, and croutons.

Before the game, the baseball dads were talking about what close calls they've had with deer on that road.

"They make poor choices," one dad said. "They're good at hiding, but they make poor choices when it comes to cars."

The first game was against a version of the Carson City team whom the Huskies have played before. It was a great day for baseball —sunny and warm—and everyone was excited to be playing in

Nevada. The Mammoth Huskies pitched well, but lost the game in the middle innings when they started throwing the ball around in panic, resulting in overthrows, errors, and runs scored by the opposition. "Oops. Snowball fight," said Coach Luke.

In the second of the doubleheader, undaunted by the size of the Carson City team, the Huskies began the game by playing out of their minds, running aggressively while the lumbering opponents stumbled over the ball or overthrew the basemen. The official word is that "we don't keep score in Fall Ball," but I think the Huskies were up by five or six runs before the giant Nevadans started getting the bat on the ball.

When we arrived in Dayton, we were surprised to see horse poop on the streets of the residential neighborhood leading into the Mark Twain Park. *Do Nevadans ride their horses through the streets?* It turns out that a herd of wild horses reside in the area, and they graze, literally, in the park. They are fenced out of the actual ball field, but they can circulate among the bleachers, grassy areas, bathrooms, parking lot, etc. They are as free to meander as the tumbleweeds that blow across the park. There is horse poop everywhere. They would occasionally start running in the field beyond the outfield, which was very distracting to the batters.

"I like horses too," shouted a coach. "But keep your eye on the ball."

In a quiet moment during the baseball game, I heard a rooster crow.

Illustration - Lake

SNOW COMES

The snow doesn't give a soft white damn whom it touches.

~ E. E. CUMMINGS

October 20–26, 2014

Monday

SOCCER SCENES: AT practice, Coach Alex strolled over and asked me if I would supervise the practice because he had to go back to work. "Just don't let them fight," he said.

During a game, there had been some discussion about a team party, and one of the mothers sighed, "We're Mexican. We'll cook for one hundred, and thirty will come." The rumor persists that one of the soccer games was rescheduled because of a *quinceañera*, a coming-out party for a Latin girl.

Tuesday

Tom is taking *two* MOOCs (massive open online courses) in bioinformatics, so our house is very quiet at night, and we watch no movies.

Wednesday

Soccer humiliation can't end. A game was suddenly scheduled for this afternoon between Yellow and Red, although it wasn't clear why.

"It will be hard for us," Coach Alex said on the phone, "but if we win, there will be another game after."

Right. Code for: *We will lose. Either immediately or immediately after.*

The game was very exciting. Red has two excellent players, including the phenomenal kicker Lexis. They have already beaten Julian's team twice in the regular season. They scored first, but our own star, Jesus, tied it up with a well-coordinated effort that resulted in our guys getting a goal. Then Yellow snuck another one in when the Red goalie bobbled a shot. This put Yellow ahead 2–1. Red kept battling and tied it up when our defense got out of position. But Yellow was on fire and executed some great teamwork and passing, and Jesus scored, putting Yellow up 3–2 at halftime.

The Red team got a thorough talking-to at halftime, and they came back on the field full of inspiration. Lexis took shot after shot that missed by inches, giving all the Yellow parents heart attacks and drawing howls of distress from the Red parents. Then early in the second half, Red made an incredible shot that flew in the goal just over our goalie's hands. Red was playing better, and the game stayed tied at 3–3. A win was looking pretty hopeless. Then, with a few minutes remaining, Yellow again and again worked the ball up the field, and Jesus finally managed to get a shot off and won the game—not that we know what happens next or why we played this game.

Tom announced that when he left our house to come to the game, he noticed a bear in our next-door neighbor's driveway. "It was just a little bear," he said.

A woman who works at Footloose Sports told us today that a man came in and bought twelve pairs of new skis, six for each of his two children. "Slalom, X-C, powder, everything," she said. There was a brief silence.

"Well, I guess money is no object for him," another mother said and sighed and plucked at the grass.

Mammoth Lakes is one of those rare places where you (well, people like me) do cross paths with the über rich, the ones who travel up here in their private jets with their pilot, chef, and masseuse and who pay for their kids to fly up each weekend to be on the ski team. As Kristen says, "They have a mansion up here and a mansion down there and probably a few other mansions around the country."

Friday

We set up another informal baseball hitting practice after school and got Jack to come with us before his cello lesson. The paper ran a photo of the violin students, including Oscar, all sitting with their bows raised. There must have been fifteen of them. Brian and Rebecca of the Felici Piano Trio are having a dramatic effect on the musical education of the local kids. Jack says he is using a cello that Brian loaned him, one that Brian played when he was growing up.

Saturday

It was a cold, windy day, and we agreed that it was time for a day off. I'm tired from my exercise program, and Julian has been busy as a bee. We watched the World Series on "tape delay," ate soup, and played chess (Julian lost all his pieces and still beat me).

October 27–November 2, 2014

Monday

The temperature is going down! It was twenty-three degrees at Chair 15 this morning on our way to school. Brrr. Snow is forecast for this weekend. Here it comes!

The Twin Lakes Campground closed this weekend, and now it is *really* quiet on my hike. The beauty of the area continues to amaze me. There were about one thousand grebes and mallards on the lower lake today. You couldn't have shoehorned another duck in there. They're either migrating or that's one hell of a bird convention. Julian stirred up a herd of deer this morning when he raced down southern Majestic Pines on his bike. As he whirred by, a group of seven or eight deer panicked and scrambled up the hillside to get away from the dark, helmeted creature on two wheels with a red blinking tail.

Julian called at noon to say that there was a soccer game this afternoon: Yellow against Will's team. It was announced over the school PA—that's how he knew. There's a convoluted rumor circulating about why this is a Mammoth-only playoff tournament. The story is that at the first playoff game with Bishop, the Bishop parents refused to sit on the proper side of the field, and the ref ruled that Bishop forfeited the game because of their insubordination. In response allegedly, Bishop refused to participate in the tournament, and the officials decreed that the four Mammoth teams would hold playoffs against each other. Which means that, despite a record of one to a-whole-bunch, Julian's team is now competing for the championship.

This would be a tough match. Remarkably, nearly all of the team members showed up despite the short notice. However, Will's team is coming off the Carson City tournament this past weekend (Cookie's

Best, as it is known) where they won three games to get into the final and finally succumbed.

The final was a good game and very well refereed by Will's dad, and Yellow played with renewed vigor and motivation. It seems clear to me now that unless you are willing to cross the ball in front of the goal, you will not win. Yellow does not share my view. They lost 0–2. At last, mercifully, soccer has come to an end (I think).

We have been enjoying the World Series games on "tape delay" all week, but they are finally over. We were (well, I was) officially rooting for the Giants, especially when watching the rookie Joe Panik play his heart out, sporting two spots of bright pink on his cheeks. But it was hard not to be secretly disappointed for the Royals and the amazing Lorenzo Cain, especially after their catcher Salvador Perez took a terrible blow on the leg and kept playing.

Thursday
With a storm bearing down upon us, we went on one last "magical wonderland ride." This time we included Mac, who turns out to be an expert mountain biker. At the start we swung out over to the slopes above Reds Meadow, which offered some gulp-worthy views down into the chasms. It made for a pretty good climb at the start. I'd never been in that area before because there are no ski runs over there. Then, at the end, instead of riding all the way over to Chair 15, we turned back and rode down the long S curves to Canyon Lodge. It was another long and spectacular two-hour ride.

Friday—Halloween!
We were running late this morning and decided to *fly* down to school on the new Meridian bike lane, beside the big new beautiful sidewalk

(thanks, Mammoth!). They're even building a substantial covered transit stop with a peaked roof. Of course, it took less than twenty-four hours before I heard a complaint about how ridiculous it was to narrow that road to two lanes to add the bike lanes.

"What *man* thought that up?" a mother complained. "You can't even pass!"

Weather is on the way! All week, Howard Sheckter, Mammoth's amateur weather forecaster, has been predicting a storm for tonight, generating great excitement in town. "We're going to get some weather!" you would hear locals say as they kept a constant eye on the sky. Preparatory scenes: a man at a nearby house was trying to start a chain saw while smoking a cigarette. Vons was abuzz, and the paper says you have to add a half hour to your planned time there because at this time of year you know everyone in the store. Kristen says she feels like she should put on a party dress before she goes grocery shopping because it's an instant social event. Tom and I rode there after school drop-off and laid in important pre-storm emergency supplies, like celery and donuts. I took a pass on the six-packs of mega-sized tubs of Spam.

Today on my hike, it looked as though someone had opened an enormous bag of cotton balls and hurled them up into the sky where they stuck in an evenly distributed array of small white puffs. The fall colors are now on the ground. A big storm cloud was brooding over Mammoth Mountain as we set off early for Halloween, heeding Howard's advice.

Trick-or-treating in Mammoth Lakes works like this: people contribute bags of Halloween candy to a communal box at Vons which gets taken to the Trails neighborhood and distributed to the homeowners. This morning, having missed the deadline at the store, Tom and I rode down to drop off bags of candy at an excessively decorated house, owned by a man who was holding four yapping Chihuahuas on leashes and who explained to us that there would be hot cocoa and cider this evening.

"Now that I'm retired, we can be here for Halloween!" he said excitedly.

At 5:00 p.m., children and parents arrived at the Trails to a wonderful horrorland of pumpkins, ghosts on wires, creepy window coverings, makeshift graveyards, and hot cider. The streets were closed, so cars were parked *everywhere*—far up Meridian on both sides of the street in all directions and up College Parkway by Cerro Coso Community College.

The decorations were amazing. Brian and Rebecca of the Felici Piano Trio had created a ghostly ensemble of skeletons playing cello, violin, and oboe in a graveyard of famous composers. Several houses were serving candies from a second story deck by funneling the goodies down a long pipe to the line of kids below. One ingenious resident lay hidden in a casket and then slowly opened the cover and rose up spookily to serve treats from a basket. Someone had built an elaborate haunted house in their garage that the kids crawled through. It was fantastic.

And the trickers rose to the occasion with fabulous costumes of warriors, bunnies, bears, swamp things, vampires, Super Mario Brothers... Kids ran around or were pulled in wagons or drove themselves; Dracula drove his miniature ATV, along with his Minecraft companion who pointed his sword and intoned, "To the next house!" after each successful candy operation.

Oscar was a gladiator, and Julian was a witch doctor complete with monocle, top hat, and a cane of skulls. Dixon was a medieval something that required a very impressive and heavy sword. He wore a bathrobe stylishly decorated with reflective duct tape. He looked great! Taff was a ninja, and Brett was unrecognizable under a lot of blood. Girls were butterflies, Superwomen, queens, cheerleaders, and other frilly things. We got back to Kristen's before eight o'clock with three big bags of candy that the boys renegotiated so that bad unappetizing fruit-based candies were turned into *chocolate*.

Saturday

Sure enough, as I write this from my loft, I look out on a winter wonderland. There were only a couple inches when I got up at 6:30 a.m., but it snowed all morning and has accumulated about six inches. Suddenly, skiing sounds really fun.

The fun continued with Oscar's birthday party at the Mammoth Rock 'n' Bowl, or the Drink 'n' Bowl as I think of it, because I always hear about people doing more drinking there than rocking. It's brand new with shiny equipment and shoes, foosball, ping-pong, and a fancy lighted bar. Business seems to be good; by evening nearly all of the twelve lanes were full, and there were quite a few people hanging out in the bar. The paper reported an incident where a woman pulled another woman's hair while she was bowling, though they were apparently unknown to each other. *Can you tick someone off just by the way you bowl?* There was no such excitement while we were there.

Upstairs, in a silent deeply carpeted area, there are three golf simulators, a golf shop, and an upscale brasserie. The attendant said business upstairs was slow this summer, but they expect it to pick up now that winter is upon us. The enterprise is the brainchild of a local married couple, both attorneys. The husband was on site, checking on customers. He looked quite attorney-esque.

Everyone bowled—kids on one lane and parents on another. After coming in last on the first game, Julian and Tom redeemed themselves: they blew by everyone on the second game and won! I choked under pressure in the second game, and Tom beat me by two points. I will require a grudge match.

And the fun goes on! Tonight was the second concert of the Felici Piano Trio series. Fewer people attended than the first concert, perhaps because of the bits of snow still on the road and geriatric fears of falls on ice. Two children were in attendance; the rest of us were either old or really old.

The concerts are an opportunity for date night in Mammoth, and there's lots of hubbub as couples greet each other and chat. I was struck by how some of the husbands and wives seem to be sick of each other. The man who stares stonily ahead while his wife maneuvers into her chair using a walker. The way a wife talks to her husband as though he were a child whose eccentric habits have to be indulged: "Now. Do you want the program. No. Fine. Do you want me to remove the staple so you can read the paper." The subtle put-downs: "I'm going to the bathroom." "I know."

There were murmurs of news about Shirley before the concert began, and Brian introduced the evening by dedicating the first piece to Shirley—a longtime devotee who usually sits in the front row but tonight was in the hospital in Reno for health reasons.

"What happened to Shirley?" someone behind me whispered.

A woman with a German accent replied, "She hat a stroke und zey didn't fint her for zree days." On that ominous note, the concert began.

They played Mozart's Piano Quartet in E-flat major, a joyful piece to help bring Shirley back to health. The addition of the viola was enjoyable although I thought it was a bit too quiet. They also played a weird and wonderful more modern piece by Frank Bridge titled the "Fantasy Quartet." The third piece was Brahms' Piano Quartet in G minor, which was extraordinary, especially the final Rondo alla Zingarese movement called the "Gypsy Rondo" with its exuberant Hungarian fiddling. I read later that it is considered one of the most difficult movements to perform of Brahms' chamber music. The quartet made it look easy, even fun—Rebecca's bow was flying!

Sunday

Terry Gross commented in a *Fresh Air* interview that people whose work requires them to hash things out in their minds constantly struggle with being mentally present because their minds are elsewhere. That observation resonated with me very much; when I am in writing mode, I find it difficult to stop writing in my mind when I am [supposed to be] doing other activities. It makes me very distracted and sometimes keeps me awake at night, as my beleaguered brain feverishly rephrases paragraphs, adjusts word choices, and tries to smooth over rough spots. I've never heard writers talk about that.

In other news:

Julian: I've noticed how many kids have piercings. Can I get one?

Mom [slow thinker]: Ah… Kids on your baseball team?

Julian: No, but about half of my soccer team.

Mom: Really?

Julian: No, only one. But a lot of kids in my school have them.

November 3–9, 2014
Monday

I slid and stumbled through my hike this morning. The snow is much deeper higher up, and the upper parts of both Old Mammoth Road and Lake Mary are closed to traffic, which makes for wonderful quiet hiking. Kristen says I need snowshoes.

Tuesday

On my hike, as I was climbing past the Valentine Reserve, a fawn stepped daintily out onto the road, peered around sniffing, and then minced its way across the road. I've seen a number of deer in that spot. It seems to be their official crossing. When I got home, I sat on the front porch for a few minutes keeping an eye on the bunny that hangs out under our cars, and then one of the omnipresent chipmunks dashed across the floor and came so close to me it nearly ran across my foot.

Wednesday

Because it gets dark early now since the time change, the last baseball practice is pulled forward to a 3:00 p.m. start. A spectacular full moon rises over the White Mountains, a Frosty Moon, lighting up blue- and rose-colored layers of clouds. The boys linger in the twilight, shagging balls and kidding around, perhaps sad to see the season end. Julian is quite cold by the time he climbs in the car, and we run the heater as we drive into the last smudges of the sunset and back to town.

Friday–Monday

Baseball has ended with a whimper. The baseball tournament scheduled for this weekend petered out because of conflicts with Soccer All-Stars and family travel plans for Veterans Day. Since Julian is out of school Monday and Tuesday, we decided to make a quick trip down to Del Mar.

Kristen warned us that being back in Southern California might be a shock: *Traffic! Noise! People! Stimulation! Culture shock!!* she texted. My reaction to being back in "civilization" was "ugh." That section on I-215 looks like an altered version of the rapture when all things of beauty have taken to the skies, leaving behind only depressing ugliness.

The weather was quite hot, and I had forgotten how lovely the air is down in Del Mar, caressing and sparkling. The climate really is idyllic: cool ocean breezes and warm sunshine. We met up with friends and had a fabulous dinner at our neighbors'. We are fortunate indeed to know such curious and smart people. If I could just get *them* to move to Mammoth...

Tuesday, November 11, 2014

We left the kindness-induced enclave, as a friend describes Del Mar, at 1:30 p.m., which we thought was a reasonable start. Little did we know.

The stop off at Trader Joe's in Temecula was madness. Four lanes of traffic jam struggling through intersections crossing four more lanes of traffic jam, and commercial horribleness as far as the eye can see. At the store, too many people trying to cram their enormous cars into tiny parking spaces, honking at each other because that always helps, and colliding into each other's shopping carts inside the crowded store. *And people choose to live here,* I thought.

Then there was a sig alert, which is Californian for "epic traffic logjam," through Cajon Pass because four lanes in both directions just aren't enough for us, so we have to crash our cars into each other. Trucks and cars were strewn up and down the freeway on both sides as people bailed out to sleep, or pee, or cry, or because their cars couldn't go anymore. Seven miles, and an hour and a half later, when we finally broke free, I found myself uttering some very bad words as I had to merge into *now-free! free-to-speed!* racing traffic to get around a car stalled in my lane. It was incredibly f***ing dangerous. At the first gas station, I was in another traffic jam at the ladies' room where the girls were all doing the pee-pee dance.

This is hell, I texted Kristen. *I cant wait 2 get home.* You know I'm desperate when I text—I never text.

I know, she wrote back instantly.

Finally, back in the peace and quiet and dark on US 395, a large silvery-tan cat floated across the highway in front of us, its graceful jump illuminated briefly in our headlights. We speculated that it was a bobcat. Sometime later, a large owl with a death wish dipped into our headlights, careering toward the car. Tom managed to avoid it, and I prayed it didn't meet its demise on the grill of the semitruck driving next to us. The dark town greeted us with a restful silence. How wonderful to be back in our home for now.

To be continued...

NOTES ON SOURCES

In the tradition of Sierra Club historian Francis P. Farquhar, to make for smoother reading when quoting others, I have on occasion omitted words or even whole sentences without using the conventional signs of omission.

In researching these stories, I was fortunate to have access to the work and wisdom of others as outlined below. Nevertheless, all errors and omissions are my own.

For the account of the search for Peter Starr, I benefited from the book by William Alsup, a federal district court judge, titled *Missing in the Minarets: The Search for Walter A. Starr, Jr.* Judge Alsup proved himself an excellent detective, sleuthing out the clues and evidence to support his reporting. His detailed and beautifully expressed text is highly recommended. Of special note are the many photographs and maps of the area, exquisitely reproduced by the Yosemite Association.

For background on Matthew Greene's disappearance, I relied on newspaper reports, notes by the searchers, including Matt's father, and his sister's extensive Facebook postings as well as personal correspondence with me. I am grateful for her willingness to answer my many questions and her support of this story.

I also drew heavily from Dean Rosnau's postings about his search activities on supertopo.com. They are worth viewing because of the extraordinary photos he uses to tell the story. Dean has just published a book about his many adventures entitled *The Shortest Straw: Search and Rescue in the High Sierra*. As predicted by the quality and sensitivity of his writing about his search for Matt, it is an exceptional and riveting book, as well as a showcase for Dean's special sense of humor.

For the details of Maverick's search effort, I consulted his postings on highsierratopix.com and appreciate his personal correspondence and conversations with me. It was very helpful and moving to understand what motivates those who search.

In reporting the events concerning the eventual cancellation of a trans-Sierra highway through Reds Meadow, I relied primarily on Jack Fisher's book *Stopping the Road*. Jack is a former physician who returned to school following his retirement to pursue a master's degree in history. I highly recommend his dramatic and original book which avidly portrays the seriousness and dedication that he brought to the task of telling this local story.

ACKNOWLEDGMENTS

All books are a team effort; this one was especially so. First, thank you to the early readers of the Mammoth Letters who suggested I keep writing about the Eastern Sierra. Without you the book wouldn't have been born. I also owe a debt of gratitude to experts who graciously reviewed early drafts for accuracy: Bob Drake, Jack Fisher, Marye Roeser, Annie Rinaldi, Jill Vanko, and John Wentworth. Many thanks are due the Southern Mono Historical Society for consultation and the book launch party. Thank you to Liza Whitmore of the Department of Transportation for talking to me about the I-80 operations.

Shields Richardson and Robert Joki fit reading advance copies of the book into their busy schedules, and special thanks to Mike Gervais of the *Mammoth Times* for publishing an early version of *Absens and Indagans* and for encouraging my writing. Heartfelt appreciation goes to Tiffany Greene and Maverick for talking to me about Matt Greene's disappearance.

Then there are the talented people who helped bring the book to fruition: my lovely editor, Melanie Astaire Witt, and wise writing and content adviser, Andy Selters, along with Damonza who created the cover and interior design. A special shout out goes to Kira Hirsch and her art teacher Melanie Taylor who created the illustrations for the book. Kira is a junior at Francis Parker High School in San Diego and destined to be a noteworthy artist.

Finally, thank you to my husband and my two sons for permitting me to write about them. As a writer, I am lucky to have them as subjects; as a human, I am just plain lucky to have them.

BIBLIOGRAPHY

Alpers, Tim. *My Sphere of Influence: A Life in Basketball*. Bozeman, MT: Companion Press, 2013.

Alsup, William. *Missing in the Minarets: The Search for Walter A. Starr, Jr.* Yosemite National Park, CA: Yosemite Association, 2001.

Austin, Mary. *The Land of Little Rain*. New York: Penguin Books, 1988. First published 1903 by Houghton Mifflin.

Bond, Michael. *A Bear Called Paddington*. New York: Collins & Son, 1958.

Cummings, E. E. *ViVa*. New York: Liveright, 1931.

Farquhar, Francis P. *History of the Sierra Nevada*. Berkeley: University of California Press, 1965.

Fisher, Jack. *Stopping the Road: The Campaign Against Another Trans-Sierra Highway*. Sager Group, 2014.

Forstenzer, Martin. *Mammoth: The Sierra Legend*. Missoula, MT: Mountain Press Publishing, 2005.

Hess, August. *The Kid from Mono Mills: Augie's Century*. San Bernadino, CA: 2016.

Hill, Mary. *Geology of the Sierra Nevada*. Berkeley: University of California. Press, 1975.

Howard, Thomas Frederick. *Sierra Crossing: First Roads to California*. Berkeley: University of California Press, 1998.

Milne, A. A. *Winnie-the-Pooh*. New York: E. P. Dutton, 1926.

Muir, John. *The Mountains of California*. New York: Century, 1894.

Reed, Adele. *Old Mammoth*. Palo Alto, CA: Genny Smith Books, 1982.

Rosnau, Dean. *The Shortest Straw: Search and Rescue in the High Sierra*. FastPencil, 2017.

Ross, Terry Gooch. *A Twin Falls*. Mammoth Lakes, CA: Two Birds Press, 2013.

Sharp, Robert P., and Allen F. Glazner. *Geology Underfoot in Death Valley and Owens Valley*. Missoula, MT: Mountain Press Publishing, 1997.

Webster, Paul. *The Mighty Sierra: Portrait of a Mountain World*. Palo Alto, CA: American West Publishing, 1972.

Whitehill, Karen, and Terry Whitehill. *Best Short Hikes in California's South Sierra*. 2nd ed. Seattle, WA: Mountaineers Books, 2003.

Woodruff, David, and Gayle Woodruff. *Tales Along El Camino Sierra*. Independence, CA: Independence Press, 2017.

INDEX